"Rajesh takes a fresh approach to describing the importance of data and data-based thinking. I think it is unique and most helpful that he is able to simplify the topic of data science. Once simplified, we are all able to think about the importance of using data more clearly to solve problems."

– Don Callahan, Executive Chairman, TIME

"Jugulum's book addresses two important trends in data science: adopting a process approach and democratizing the process. Appropriate for the topic, it addresses the issues in an accessible, conversational fashion. It's a rare book that is both easy and important to read."

– Thomas H. Davenport, Distinguished Professor, Babson
College and Visiting Professor,
Oxford Saïd Business School,
Fellow, MIT Initiative on the Digital Economy,
Author of Competing on Analytics *and* The AI Advantage

"While it lacks the hype of 'Machine Learning' and 'Artificial Intelligence', understanding the potential for Data Science to extract insights from structured and unstructured data is critical to virtually every skilled occupation, and to every investor. By adopting a conversational approach, Rajesh introduces data science in an informal yet informative manner and brings the field comfortably within the reach of readers without an engineering, maths, or computer science background."

– Gareth Genner, CEO and Group General Counsel,
Trust Stamp

"A fresh approach to data science, making the concepts clear through an informal conversational style. This book simplifies this critical approach in business and makes it understandable to the layperson, even without a mathematical background."

– Desh Deshpande, Entrepreneur,
Life member MIT Corporation

"I don't know how many times in my career I have heard 'if I could only do what the big corporations do and apply that to my small business I could really grow'. Rajesh has done that here. He has taken data science down to a level that anyone can use. He has helped eliminate the 'If I could only'."

– *Sandra Harry, Chairman of the Board,*
Dr. Mikel J Harry Six Sigma Management Institute Inc.,
Chief Executive Officer, The Great Discovery, LLC

"Dr. Jugulum brings deep knowledge of data science and analytics to anyone interested in understanding the 'why' and 'how' of data analytics. Common Data Sense for Professionals shows through example how data science should be approached and why it is necessary to solve common business problems in today's economic climate. Those who do not understand and practice data analytics are doomed to business failure in our increasingly connected world. Dr. Jugulum clearly shows us the path to success regardless of the type of business we are conducting. This book should be required reading for all business operators, both large and small."

– *Julianna Lindsey MD MBA, CEO/CMO,*
Radiant Precision Medicine

"Rajesh outlines a clear process approach to analyze data and make results available. Once data scientists and 'non data scientists' alike understand the results, a conversation leading actionable decisions can be made. Great read."

– *Mark Prince, MD MBA,*
Director of Inpatient Gastroenterology, GI Hospital Group

"Data science and analytics can be an overwhelming and complex topic to many readers, yet, in his book, Rajesh is able to break this down into very digestible concepts. The book follows the interaction and conversation between the two main characters, all the while delivering a foundational approach to data analysis and problem solving. A fast, enjoyable read, this book really helps to shed light on how easy it is to apply data science to solving everyday problems."

– *Dan Duzan, MD, Board Certified Internist/Hospitals*

"Data science has made great strides in helping businesses solve important problems. But still, too often business people and data scientists have a hard time working together because they come from two very different worlds. The fanciful perception of data science and AI as 'magic wands' which can be waved at problems to solve them hasn't helped. In Common Data Sense for Professionals, Rajesh Jugulum has de-mystified data science for non-technical people. His focus on problem solving with sound process management practices places data science in its proper place…as a vast and useful toolkit that, properly used, can work wonders."

– Heather H. Wilson, CEO, CLARA Analytics

"Now more than ever, we need to be guided by data, science, and facts to make informed decisions. In his new book, Common Data Sense for Professionals, Rajesh Jugulum seeks to demystify the world of data science for the layperson. As Thomas Redman notes in the Foreword to the book, 'Slowly perhaps, but inexorably, data are invading every aspect of our personal, public, and business lives.'. This book represents a helpful step forward for those seeking to understand the role of data science in the world today."

– Randy Bean, Author of Fail Fast, Learn Fast: Lessons *in Data-Driven Leadership in an Age of Disruption, Big Data, and AI, Founder and CEO, NewVantage Partners LLC*

"In this book, Rajesh finds a very systematic way to understand the problem at hand and methodically steps through relevant data collection and a structured way to solve the problem. He uses a conversational method to introduce complex concepts that makes it easy to understand. A must read for anyone who wants to understand data science."

– Gyan Dwibedy, Chief Data and Analytics Officer, Molina Healthcare

"Rajesh Jugulum has produced a jem! In the Overview, he states: 'The goal of this book is to help regular people feel at ease, in order for them to use data-based thinking and solve data-related problems.' He has thoroughly succeeded! Through the use of a hypothetical, conversational case study, much in the vein of The Goal, Jugulum demonstrates that data science is not limited to 'specialists' with advanced degrees, but is rather a way of thinking that is needed by everyone. I particularly applaud his emphasis on carefully understanding the problem one is trying to solve before jumping into analysis; a critical point often overlooked in the technical literature. Highly recommended."

– Roger Hoerl, Brate-Peschel Associate Professor of Statistics, Union College

"In his book, Rajesh Jugulum walks the readers through the 'analytic thinking' required for generating insights for informed decision making. Through a systematic approach that includes formulating problems, structuring data collection, and analyzing relevant data, he shows how one can easily solve data science problems. Addressing the topics in the form of a conversation between a mentor and a mentee engages readers. It is a must-read for anyone interested in becoming a data scientist."

– Raj Echambadi, President,
Illinois Institute of Technology

"Data has become one of the most valuable resources we have in the Information Age. Until now, the ability to extract the real value contained within this resource has been limited to a rare group of data scientists and PhDs. In Common Data Sense for Professionals, Jugulum demystifies the effective analysis of data in a way that democratizes it making it possible for a wide range of roles and personas to make informed business decisions."

– Charlie Guyer, Founder, Guyer Group

"I was delighted by how clearly Rajesh demystifies the practice of data science and dismantles the misconceived notion that all data science must be difficult or complex. The casual, conversational narrative quickly held my attention while providing a stage for exploring real world applications. As a data science practitioner, I use data in every aspect of my professional life to solve business problems. After reading Common Data Sense for Professionals, I'm reminded that not every problem we, as individuals, face is business related. With the vast access individuals have to data recording devices in the present day, or even plain paper and pencil, the process Rajesh outlines can be applied just as easily at home to improve every aspect of our lives where a problem can be found."

– Christopher Heien, Senior Data Scientist, Evernorth

"Solving problems and answering questions through analysis is typical procedure in data science. Data science involves experimenting by constructing models to predict outcomes or discover new information. Do you want to explore the realm of the latest developments in the data world? Are you considering a career in which data science is significant? Do you want to expand your knowledge? Whatever your purpose, in his book 'Common Data Sense for Professionals -Process Oriented Approach for Data Science Projects', Rajesh Jugulum has given us an interactive simple discourse to help non-technical consumers comprehend the use of data in overcoming real life challenges."

– Ahmed Ankit, Dean,
School of Business and Quality Management, HBMSU, Dubai

Common Data Sense for Professionals

Common Data Sense for Professionals

Professionals
A Process-Oriented Approach for Data-Science Projects

Rajesh Jugulum

Routledge
Taylor & Francis Group

A PRODUCTIVITY PRESS BOOK

First Published 2022
by Routledge
605 Third Avenue, New York, NY 10158

and by Routledge
4 Park Square, Milton Park, Abingdon, Oxon, OX14 4RN

Routledge is an imprint of the Taylor & Francis Group, an informa business

© 2022 Rajesh Jugulum

Library of Congress Cataloging-in-Publication Data
A catalog record for this title has been requested

ISBN: 978-0-367-76050-2 (hbk)
ISBN: 978-0-367-76048-9 (pbk)
ISBN: 978-1-003-16527-9 (ebk)

DOI: 10.4324/9781003165279

Typeset in Minion
by codeMantra

"Statistical thinking will one day be as necessary for efficient citizenship as the ability to read and write" – H.G. Wells (Source: Rao, 1989)

Contents

Foreword

Rajesh Jugulum begins this fine volume quoting H. G. Wells:

> *"Statistical thinking will one day be as necessary for efficient citizenship as the ability to read and write."* (Source: Rao, 1989)

What a prescient observation. Slowly perhaps, but inexorably, data are invading every aspect of our personal, public, and business lives.

As I write these words, billions of people will soon be in need to address some very important questions: Should I be inoculated for Covid? How about my children? If yes, which vaccine?

Their answers to these questions will have enormous personal and public health implications. And people must make their decisions amid a veritable tidal wave of information, misinformation, opinion, and politics. How to think it through? How to separate the relevant from the irrelevant, the correct from the incorrect, the helpful from the ridiculous? And who to trust?

One could easily replace "efficient citizenship" with "capable workforce" in the Wells quote. Virtually every job requires people who can create better data, develop deeper insights, and work with others to understand and leverage an increasingly diverse collection of data. And what's true for individuals is true for companies and the entire economy as well.

No surprise that many people today are calling for investments in data literacy. From where I sit only a few of these calls go far enough. Learning about data should start in preschool and command the same level of effort as teaching children, then teens, and finally adults to read and write. It is almost certainly the most important education challenge of this generation.

This introduction brings me back to Rajesh's book. The "text" stems from the premise that data science is not some sort of black magic reserved for those with advanced degrees. Rather, it is for everyone. Nor is data science simply a collection of techniques for combing through data. Rather, it is a way of thinking; a way of articulating problems; gathering, organizing, and analyzing relevant data; reaching fresh conclusions; and putting those conclusions to work. There is a method to the madness, a process for doing this work that practically anyone can learn and follow. You might have heard of it it is called the "scientific method." This is a really big deal!

One of Rajesh's main characters, Manju, reveals this process, step-by-step, as she helps Jim apply it. There is a certain beauty and elegance here. Rather than advising Jim to dive into the data, she first forces him to think deeply about the problem he wishes to solve. It sounds obvious, but I find that too many people, even professional data scientists, don't spend enough time thinking clearly about the problem they aim to solve.

There is also a critical "subtext" to this book. It stems from two observations:

1. Many people are afraid of data and data science and
2. Most people derive great joy when they complete data science projects and see the results of their labor in action!

The book also traces Jim's initial fear, the way Manju puts his mind at ease, and the fun he has doing the work. Manju is a role model for data scientists who wish to extend their influence and Jim for those who fear they may be left behind.

One final point. More than anything else, success in data science depends on talent. Many will conclude that to mean world-class data scientists. In my view, it is far more complex than that. Everyone, quite literally everyone, needs to do more with data. Said differently, why let the professional data scientists have all the fun!

Score one for those tackling the most important education issue of our generation. And score one for Rajesh Jugulum. Well done!

Thomas C. Redman, PhD
"the Data Doc"
Rumson, NJ

Preface

Data is an intrinsic part of our daily lives. Nowadays, we deal with data more closely than ever starting from the time we wake up in the morning to the time when we go to bed. Everything we do is a data point, data points that are recorded with the intent to help us lead more efficient lives. We have apps that track our workouts, sleep, food intake, personal finance, etc. We use data to impact our lives based on goals we have set for ourselves.

Businesses are starting to treat data as an important asset and doing many things with data on a much larger scale. The jump from personal data usage for self-betterment to data analysis to solve real-life business problems often feels bigger to us than it really is. In turn we often think that solving those problems requires data science tools held only by advanced degree holders, yet that is a mere misconception. Although advanced degrees are valuable, they are not a requirement to adequately run a data science project. The aim of this book is to drive out such fear/insecurity in regular people and help them solve data-related problems. Because we constantly deal with data in all walks of life, data-related thinking is extremely important for every individual to make well-informed decisions. The words of H.G. Wells regarding data-based thinking are important in this current data-driven world more than ever. In-line with Wells's thinking, the book is aimed at making regular people feel at ease for using data-based thinking to solve problems and take appropriate decisions.

Since we are all already data users, with a good game plan and with the help of software programs, anyone can solve data science problems and, in the process, can become a data scientist if they are interested. The process laid out in this book will help empower individuals to confidently work on data-related challenges so that they can become citizens of data world.

To solve data-related problems, there is a need for good problem definition, goal statement, and structure. Additionally, it is important to ensure data is fit for the intended use, consider the risk and uncertainties that exist, and use suitable analytical models or frameworks. This book discusses all these ideas in the context of solving data science problems.

The data science problems can be solved with an approach that is executed in three phases. The phases and game plans are designed to help you and your organization, no matter how small or large, run a successful data science project. Whether you are at a large company with a data management division or a small independent business with little to no data science experience, it is hoped that this book serves as a helpful guide to get the results you desire.

The book is intended to feel conversational. To do so, a fictional situation is created using a restaurant chain, called Eat Healthy and characters (Manju and Jim) to guide you through the principles and game plans illustrated in this book. Through these illustrations, Manju tries to accomplish two aims of the book – drive out fear/insecurity in Jim who does not have data science background and make regular people like Jim feel at ease for using data-based thinking to solve problems. Throughout the book, the Eat Healthy example is used to demonstrate the importance of these principles and game plans, and how they are eventually used to solve the problem at hand. In addition, the book also provides other case studies that display how the overall approach provided in the book is useful to solve real-world problems.

Hopefully, readers will enjoy this book and they will be able to adapt to data-based thinking and solve data-related problems on their own without any hesitation or fear, realizing that they can also become data scientists if they wish. If this is accomplished, then the book will have served its purpose.

Finally, I would like to conclude by acknowledging and thanking all the people and organizations that have contributed to the field of data. Here, I am reminded of famous words in Telugu language by a famous Indian Saint-Composer, Tyagayya "Endero Mahanubavulu; Andariki Vandanamulu" –meaning there are so many great people; I salute them all.

Rajesh Jugulum

Acknowledgments

I have been thinking about writing a book on data science for the regular person for quite some time. When I mentioned this idea to Tom Redman, immediately he told me this is a good idea, and this will be an important book. I would like to sincerely thank Tom for giving me early vote of confidence and for his support and encouragement during this effort and for writing the foreword. Tom provided a lot of feedback on the book's content and he also generously allowed me to use some of his materials on data quality.

I am very grateful to the following individuals (in no particular order) for their support and help during this effort by reading the manuscript of this book and endorsing the ideas.

Don Callahan	Heather H. Wilson
Thomas H. Davenport	Randy Bean
Gareth Genner	Gyan Dwibedy
Desh Deshpande	Roger Hoerl
Sandra Harry	Raj Echambadi
Julianna Lindsey	Charlie Guyer
Mark Prince	Ahmed Ankit
Dan Duzan	Christopher Heien

I would like to thank Nikhil Deshpande for carefully editing various versions of the manuscript and providing many useful suggestions. I am also thankful to Aaroh Jugulum for his help in reading the manuscript and making necessary changes.

I am very grateful to Michael Sinocchi of Productivity Press for giving me the opportunity to publish this book. When I approached Michael, he saw the value and importance of this book idea and immediately started the publication process. I am also thankful to Todd Perry of Taylor & Francis Group and Sathya Devi of the Codemantra for their patience and giving necessary time during various stages of the publication process. My special thanks to all the individuals who relentlessly contributed/are contributing to the field of data. Finally, I would like to thank my entire family for their cooperation, understanding and support throughout this effort.

OVERVIEW

What Do Data Scientists Do?

Data scientists are people within an organization who take data, analyze it, and create models to help solve problems. You may have heard of companies having data management teams, or chief information officers (CIOs) or chief data officers (CDOs), etc. They work with data, but their function is more related to vetting data and preparing it for use by data scientists.

The Goal of This Book

The goal of this book is to help regular people feel at ease in order for them to use data-based thinking and solve data-related problems. For the sake of explanation, throughout the book, a fictional restaurant chain, "Eat Healthy," is used to illustrate how various topics discussed can be applied. A basic background of the company is provided and the chapters in the book will use this example as a way of seeing the topics applied.

Background on "Eat Healthy"

Eat Healthy is a fictional east coast restaurant chain that has begun introducing plant-based food options to their existing menu. The company wants to understand why after six months, a few locations have failed to attract customers for the newly introduced items while others have succeeded. The company has twenty-five restaurants, of which twenty locations are doing well.

Using sales data, they found that these twenty locations, on an average, have increased their overall sales by 7.5% through the introduction of plant-based food items. The remaining five locations have not reached that number. Their sales, on an average, went up by only 3.7%. The company intends to improve sales in these five locations by using data science approach.

Data Science Project Roadmap

All data science projects can be broken up into three phases with game plans in each phase. The phases and game plans are designed to help your organization, no matter how small or large, run successful data science projects. Whether you are at a large company with a data management division or a small independent business with little to no data science experience, it is hoped that this book serves as a helpful guide to get the results you need.

Data Science Roadmap

Phase 1: Understanding the problem
Game plan: Problem definition, goal setting, organizational cohesion, and measurement
Phase 2: Analyzing the problem and collecting data
Game plan: Deep dive analysis, data identification and collection, and understanding the risk and uncertainty
Phase 3: Creating and analyzing models
Game plan: Data analysis, model selection, and outcome analysis

Final Note

Although this book is intended to help regular people by providing a step-by-step guide with simple game plans/strategies, it is important to have the right tools. The later chapters of the book will address data collection, model building, and analysis of data. In order to properly analyze data and begin model building, you will need access to data analytics software programs. The software will help you sort through your data and manipulate your data in order to gather insights. The choice of your software has no influence on the overall data science process.

Author

Rajesh Jugulum, PhD, is a data science, analytics, and process engineering leader. He has vast experience in these areas and held executive positions in large corporations related to healthcare and finance. Before joining industry, Rajesh was at Massachusetts Institute of Technology (MIT), where he was involved in research in the area of robust design. Currently, Rajesh is on the Board of a cloud based data science/analytics firm. He also teaches at Northeastern University, Boston as an affiliate professor.

Rajesh is the author/co-author of several papers and five books including books on robust quality, data quality, and design for lean six sigma. Rajesh also holds two US patents. Rajesh is a Fellow of American Society for Quality (ASQ) and his honors include ASQ's Feigenbaum Medal and International Technology Institute's Rockwell Medal.

1

The Meeting of Manju and Jim

Jim works in the marketing department at Eat Healthy, a fictional east-coast restaurant chain that has recently introduced various plant-based menu options. Manju is Jim's mentor. She and Jim meet frequently to discuss ideas.

Manju: Jim! It's great to see you.

Jim: Hey, Manju. Good to see you as well.

Manju: How are things? Hope all is well.

Jim: Manju, to be honest, it's been a tough couple of weeks at work.

Manju: Oh, I am so sorry to hear that. What exactly has happened?

Jim: So, we introduced a few plant-based menu items across all of our locations and for the most part, the locations have increased sales by 7.5% after their introduction, but we have five locations with pretty bad sales numbers. I guess vegetarianism isn't too popular there.

Manju: Oh. No. What was the reason for introducing plant-based items?

Jim: There are a couple of reasons – (1) our competitors have started offering plant-based options and so it became quite important for us to introduce these items to remain competitive in the market; (2) a lot of people are moving toward vegetarian options due to health concerns and offering these items helps us maintain our credibility of serving healthy options.

Manju: When did you introduce plant-based items on the menu?

Jim: Couple of quarters (six months) ago.

Manju: Do you know what are the sales numbers associated with those five locations?

DOI: 10.4324/9781003165279-1

Jim: On an average, these five locations have sales increase of 3.7%, which is considered bad since we had higher expectations. Now our challenge is to increase sales of these five locations by 7.5%.

Manju: Why only by 7.5%? Why not more?

Jim: I know increase of 7.5% may not be the best but it's much better than what our underperforming locations have done so far. Once we achieve 7.5% growth at all locations, we can focus on further growth.

Manju: Makes sense. How many locations have sales increase of 7.5%?

Jim: There are twenty locations.

Manju: Do you know why those five locations are not performing well compared to those twenty performing locations?

Jim: Exactly! We have no idea. I mean, we have guesses, but we don't want to spend money to fix a problem without knowing what the problem is.

Manju: These are new items that are added to existing list of options (including meat-based options), right?

Jim: Correct.

Manju: Do you have any data to look at?

Jim: I knew you would ask that Manju. This is the thing that has given me the most anxiety over the past few weeks. Of course, I can look at the data, but the company wants to go a step further by hiring data experts to run a data science project. These experts would be doing a big part of my job. I don't know that the company will even need me if they have data scientists performing virtually the same tasks.

Manju: Look, experts would be helpful, but you don't need experts to run a data science project. You could do it if you wanted.

Jim: I'm not a numbers guy. That's my problem.

Manju: The biggest misconception about data science is that you have to be a numbers guy to do it. To be honest, a software program or, more precisely, a statistical analysis package does a lot of the math for you.

Jim: Oh, I see. I haven't heard anything like this before. Sounds so good to my ears.

Manju: Coming back to my earlier question, do you have data to look at?

Jim: What type of data?

Manju: Sales numbers in the last quarter (past three months) for all locations. I want to see how these numbers are distributed.

Jim: I think I can get these numbers easily.

Manju: Great. Jim, remember it is important to have "the right data" for data science projects and that "data should be right." The second part "data should be right" is exactly what it sounds like: is the data correct?. The "right data" is a bit subtler. Ask yourself "Is this the best data to answer our questions?" If you don't have the right data on hand, it is important to find or collect new data which pertains to the situation. From your sales data, we can look at the distribution and check if sales increase numbers of all performing locations are in the vicinity of 7.5% or not. I also want to see if sales of all non-performing locations are isolated from those of performing locations.

Jim: Sure, Manju. I can get this data.

Manju: Excellent, Jim.

Jim: Manju, you mentioned two important aspects of the data. I understand "data should be right" part. For "the right data," how do we ensure that the data is right and who is responsible?

Manju: Great question Jim. In your case, you are responsible for sales data. What I mean is, for sales data, your sales team is responsible. They are the data users. Data users are the best people to know what is the right data to measure overall sales. This is true with all other functions. The regular business people who deal with data in their respective areas will know what data is needed for their work. If the right data is not available, it has to be collected. Having the wrong data presents a huge risk to the organizations. Sometimes, "the right data" part can also be addressed through a good problem statement that describes problem at hand very clearly. Once we know what data is needed and obtain it, then we need to understand impacting factors causing the problem (in your case – impacting factors causing poor sales). After identifying those impacting factors, we need to make sure we have right data on those factors to perform root cause analysis. For these factors, we also need to ensure data quality. One last thing: people sometimes use the phrase "fitness for use." That just means you have the right data and that data is right *(Source: Redman, 2021).* The concept of "fitness for use" was introduced by Dr. J.M.Juran, a famous quality expert *(Source:* Redman, 2021).

Jim: Thanks Manju. This is really getting very interesting. Also, based on what you told earlier, one need not be a numbers guy to run data science projects, right?

Manju: Yes. That's what I meant.

Jim: So what does a data scientist do?

Manju: I can teach you if you want.

Jim: Now?

Manju: Yes. That's how simple it is. Data science is more about structure and organizational cohesion than math. One should have some experience in understanding real-world problems. Here, let me recall a quote from a great Indian saint Swami Vivekananda:

> *Knowledge can only be got in one way, the way of experience; there is no other way to know.*
>
> (*Source:* VivekaVani, 2019)

So, with your experience you can easily solve data science problems.

Jim: That sounds so good, Manju. I agree experience is critical for solving real-world problems. But, still I am concerned about math part.

Manju: Don't worry. I'll explain the meaning behind the math, but you don't need to get in the weeds with the math to run a successful data science project.

Jim: …Ok, let's do it!

Manju: Just to preface, to run any data science project, I would propose three main phases that can be carried out with different game plans.

Phase 1: Understanding the problem
  Game plan: Problem definition, goal setting, organizational cohesion, and measurement

Phase 2: Analyzing the problem and collecting data
  Game plan: Deep dive analysis, data identification and collection, and understanding the risk and uncertainty

Phase 3: Creating and analyzing models
  Game plan: Data analysis, model selection, and outcome analysis

Jim: These are really interesting phases and just common sense.

Manju: That is exactly correct. Keep thinking about these phases and game plan. We will continue this discussion again in a week when you get the data on sales for all locations. Please prepare a bar graph using the data. Actually, I want you to prepare a bar graph by separating performing and non-performing locations. This will help us to clearly define the problem you are facing.

Jim: Okay. I will collect the data and be ready for our session next week? Do you prefer same day around same time?

Manju: Yes. That works for me.

(Jim collects data and completes bar graph analysis. He meets with Manju one week later).

Manju: Hey, Jim. How are you?

Jim: Fine, Manju. I prepared the bar graph for the data as you suggested.

Manju: Excellent. Let's take a look at it.

Jim: Here is the bar graph in Figure 1.1.

Manju: Wonderful. If we look at this graph, what can you tell Jim?

Jim: I think there is a clear separation between performing locations and non-performing locations. I also calculated averages. The average sales increase for performing locations is 7.5% and that for non-performing locations is 3.7%

Manju: Great. These numbers are matching with what you told me last week. Thanks for validating them. We can also make one more observation – performing locations are all performing by and large at the same level without much variation and same is true for non-performing locations as well. Do you agree?

Jim: Absolutely.

Manju: Let me quickly perform one more analysis by constructing a histogram for these locations. Histogram is also a type of bar graph, which shows how the data points are distributed or spread across. Unlike in the bar graph that you prepared, in histograms, we use the values (in our case % sales increase) along x-axis and frequencies along y-axis. Frequencies here correspond to number of values of sales % increase between 3 and 4, 4 and 5, 5 and 6, 6 and 7, and so on.

Manju: Did you get that?

Jim: Yes, Manju.

Manju: If we connect all the bars with a curve, we can approximate the distributions to some known distributions such as normal distribution. Do you know what is normal distribution?

Jim: Yes. I do. It is a bell-shaped curve. Do not ask me anything beyond this.

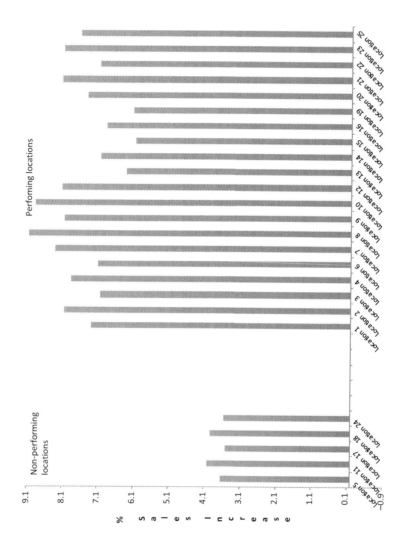

FIGURE 1.1

Bar graph for sales data (performing and non-performing locations separated).

Manju: Okay, Jim. Don't get nervous. All I want to see is whether these locations' data follow a normal distribution or not. Let me use excel program to perform histogram analysis.

(Manju takes few minutes to perform histogram analysis).

Manju: Here you go. The histogram for all locations is as shown in Figure 1.2. What do you think Jim?

Jim: I am looking at the line connecting the bars. I think it does not look like normal distribution.

Manju: Awesome. That is correct. If you look at entire data considering all locations, the data does not form a normal distribution. However, if you see the line connecting only performing locations, we can see a normal distribution. Do you agree?

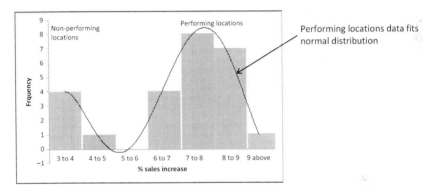

FIGURE 1.2
Histogram analysis for % sales data.

Jim: Yes. I do. Thanks, Manju.

Manju: No problem. Further, we can say that the performing locations are predictable because they follow a specific distributional pattern. According to Dr. Shewhart's process control theory, observations with normal distribution can be used to ensure statistical control. Also, since the average sales increase of performing locations is 7.5%, we can use this as the target for all non-performing locations.

Jim: I heard about Dr. Shewhart in one of the training classes that I attended.

Manju: He was a great scientist and came up with idea of statistical control. We will talk about his contributions and the terms related to "control" and "out of control" later when we discuss process control aspects.

Jim: Okay. Also, I am not understating why you said that performing locations are predictable.

Manju: Good question Jim. I did not want to get into these things now as I was planning on explaining later when we start discussing process control aspects. However, let me explain this quickly. According to statistical process control, as introduced by Dr. Shewhart, if a set of observations from a process form a normal distribution, then the process is said to be predictable, and this set of observations can be used for ensuring process control.

Jim: Oh. I see.

Manju: If a process is in control, the observations will lie between three standard deviations from the mean or average value on either side. Furthermore, if a value is beyond three standard deviations from the average value, it is out of control and this observation causes variation in the performance.

Jim: Hold on, Manju. I have a basic question. I understand the term average but what I struggle to understand is standard deviation. Can you explain standard deviation in simple terms?

Manju: Okay. I will try my best. Standard deviation is a measure of variation. The width of normal distribution shows how much variation exists in a process. Look at Figure 1.3, which shows variation for % of sales increase for performing locations of Eat Healthy. The numbers vary between 6.04% and 9.04% and average is at 7.5%. Here note that, 6.04%–9.04% provides the range of distribution of points. This represents overall deviation (variation) in the process. On the other hand, standard deviation gives us a measure that represents deviation of all observations (in this case % sales increase values) from the average, which is 7.5%. Standard deviation also indicates consistency of values. Higher deviation means more variation and lower deviation means more consistency.

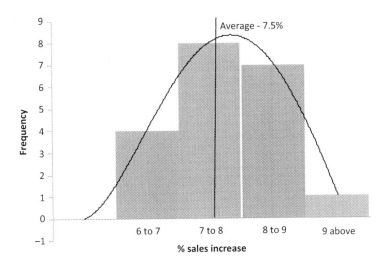

FIGURE 1.3
Description of variation with performing locations data.

Jim: Thanks, Manju. It is now clear to me.

Manju: Glad to help. The idea of standard deviation can be murky, so it was good to clarify such a crucial topic. Now, let us get back to our discussion. For the performing locations, the average is 7.5 and standard deviation is 0.84. The lower limit will be 7.5 minus 3 times 0.84, which is 4.98%. So any value less than 4.98% is out of control. For non-performing locations, all values are less than 4.98% and they are out of control as compared to performing locations. On the other hand, the minimum sales increase % for performing locations is 6.04% indicating that all performing locations are in control. Got it?

Jim: Yes, Manju. I guess you will touch upon this concept later as well, right?

Manju: Yes. I will explain this in detail when we start our discussion about statistical control.

Jim: Great. Now, I am anxious to learn about the data science strategies.

Manju: Let's dive right into them!

Jim: Let's do it!

2

Understanding the Problem

PHASE 1

Game Plan: Problem Definition, Goal Setting, Organizational Cohesion, and Measurement

Manju: Let me start with phase 1 of data science problem-solving approach by focusing on problem definition first.

Problem Definition

Every organization has something they are looking to change or improve, it could be client retention, improving cycle times, increasing sales, etc. This step in the data science process is to sim-

> If I had only one hour to save the world, I would spend fifty-five minutes defining the problem, and only five minutes finding the solution
> **– Albert Einstein (Source: AZ quotes)**

ply describe the problem in a clear and concise manner, thus communicating the core issue. In my opinion, most organizations will not get to this stage or will struggle to get to this stage. Due to this, the process of addressing the issue is often unorganized and undefined resulting in the problem persisting and the organizations have to restart the process of addressing it. This cycle is all too common for many workplaces that do not use the principles of data science as the basis of their problem solving. The usefulness of data science then is in identifying a problem and learning how to properly address it. It is the creation and execution of a clear plan with checks and balances, milestones, and a timeline that is crucial in ensuring the success of your data science project.

DOI: 10.4324/9781003165279-2

You can probably guess that Eat Healthy is looking to solve the discrepancy in sales between their twenty performing locations and their five non-performing locations.

Jim: Yes. So, what will be a good problem statement for us?

Manju: That is what I am going to discuss now. Jim, based on the information you provided, if we have two problem statements as stated below, which one you think correctly describes your problem?

Problem statement (a): "Eat Healthy has introduced plant-based items in all twenty five locations to maintain their credibility of serving healthy food options. Data shows that twenty locations have increased sales by 7.5% and the remaining five locations have increased only by 3.7%. So it is important to understand the factors, also known as drivers, that are deterrents to the adoption of plant-based items resulting in poor sales in the five non-performing locations and take proper actions to increases the sales by at least 7.5% in these locations."

Problem statement (b): "Six months ago, Eat Healthy has introduced plant-based items in all twenty five locations to remain competitive in their market space and maintain their credibility of serving healthy food options. Analysis of last quarter's data shows that twenty locations have increased sales by 7.5% and the remaining five locations have increased only by 3.7%. So it is important to understand the factors, also known as drivers, that are deterrents to the adoption of plant-based items resulting in poor sales in the five non-performing locations and take proper actions to increases the sales by at least 7.5% in these locations."

Jim: Manju, I think problem statement (b) is the more accurate description of our problem.

Manju: I agree with you, Jim. Problem statement (b) provides details about the time factor when the plant-based items were introduced and time period corresponding to the data. In addition, this statement also describes competition, which is also an important reason for the introduction of plant-based items.

Jim: Got it. I recall one famous data expert saying "generally people with PhD's or good experience will come up with better problem statement than others." I think your experience is helping describe problem accurately.

Manju: I am not so sure about that. Let's now discuss goal setting.

Goal Setting

Like problem definition, goals must be clearly defined and communicated. Simply stating that the goal of Eat Healthy is to increase sales is not enough. Goals and subsequently your goal statement should be Specific (to the point), Measurable, Doable (Attainable), Realistic, and should have Time aspect (time to achieve the goal). Proper use of these aspects will result in the creation of a clear goal statement.

Jim: So an appropriate goal statement for Eat Healthy could read something like this: *Improve the sales in our five non-performing locations by 7.5%.*

Manju: Your goal statement would be perfect if you add a time component to it. In addition, we can also aim for higher than 7.5% sales increase as higher sales is always preferred. So, I think your goal statement would be better if it is read like this: **Improve the sales in our five non-performing locations by at least 7.5% in a period of six months.**

This goal statement is specific, measurable, and time-based. What constitutes as realistic and doable is largely dependent on specific organization but for the sake of this example, let's assume increasing sales by at least 7.5% in six months is possible for Eat Healthy. This goal statement clearly communicates to everyone involved in what the organization would consider a successful project.

Jim: I agree. That makes sense. Adding time component is really important.

Manju: Thanks, Jim. Let's move onto organizational cohesion.

Organizational Cohesion

Now that we have a clearly defined problem and goal, we must begin communicating how to address it and who will be involved. Jim, how do you run projects within your company?

Jim: To run a project, we typically start with creating a project charter with objectives, resources, roles, etc.

Manju: Great! Many companies use project charters to make sure there is cohesion within the organization. The project charter will formally establish the scope, objectives, resources, expected business value, role clarity, timeframes, and core deliverables. In Figure 2.1, you can see a sample project charter. Does your charter look like this?

Jim: Yes, it is somewhat similar though the format is different. I think the project charter is a pretty common tool that brings all relevant people together in order to accomplish the goal.

Manju: Exactly. Note that a project charter is very important to run a project. Based on this, usually, a project plan will be developed with deliverables and associated timelines and a project manager will be responsible for running the project and making sure that all deliverables are delivered as per timelines.

Jim: Exactly. That is similar to how we operate.

Manju: Okay great. Now let me start discussing measurement strategy.

Measurement

Measurement is how we address ambiguity in a data science project. Knowing what to measure is often the difference between making the right decision or the wrong decision. Suppose someone with high blood pressure is feeling

> Measure, measure, measure.
> Measure again and again to find out the difference and the difference of the difference
> **–Galileo (Source: Rao, 1989)**

dizzy. Most people would attribute the dizziness to the high blood pressure and search for solutions with that as the underlying cause. Suppose you then measure the person's blood pressure and it reads normal. If you had taken actions to combat the dizziness with high blood pressure as the underlying cause, you would likely not improve the situation. In fact, you may be hurting it.

Jim: Yes. It makes lot of sense. We need to attack the right causes.

Manju: You are correct. Measuring helps us understand what the underlying problems may be and also provides us direction to begin solving them.

Charter Element	Description	Comments
Project Goal	Clear goal statement with a success mesaure. Goal should be Specific, Measurable, Doable, Realistic and Time based	
Scope	Project scope should include processes, tools, systems, and data that will be included. Primary metric:	
Team members/Roles	List team members and and define associated roles.	
Resources	Estimate of resources that are needed	

Phase	Major deliverables	Date
Phase 1	Project major deliverables with various phases and timelines	dd/mm
Phase 2		dd/mm
Phase 3		dd/mm

FIGURE 2.1
Sample project charter.

When we make strategic decisions in a data science project, we want to continually measure the results to ensure we are moving toward our target.

So how do we measure our strategic decisions? For any metric, we should be considering the following three aspects (Figure 2.2):

1. Target: This indicates target performance level, which is the ultimate destination;
2. Capability: Attainable performance level, after removing the sources of variation;
3. Actual: Actual performance level in the presence of variation.

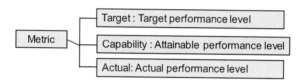

FIGURE 2.2
Different aspects of a metric.

Jim: Manju, I am assuming you are going to explain these terms in detail?

Manju: Of Course. Before we move forward, I should define the terms listed above. Target refers to the target level of performance. Target setting is to be done by business experts, through historical data analysis and comparisons with best in class. Capability refers to your ability to reach a particular level without any variation. Capability refers to attainable level of performance. Actual refers to the level of performance in an existing situation (in the presence of variation). Please note that most often the actual performance level is less than capability, because of inevitable nature of variation. We cannot eliminate effect of variation completely; we can only minimize it. As famous quality expert, W.E. Deming, aptly put:

> *Variation is life; or life is variation.*
> (*Source:* Deming, 1993)

So, we have to live with variation.

Jim: Okay, Manju. Can you explain a bit more about variation and causes of variation?

Manju: Sure, Jim. Variation usually comes from two sources special causes and common causes. Simply put, special cause variation describes unique external factors that may cause a shift in the process or system. Common cause variation describes a cause inherent to the system being measured. Weather is good example of a special cause. For example, if it snows heavily during a football game, the quarterback (QB)'s performance may drop significantly since the conditions affect QB's accuracy. On the other hand, if someone has to become a great QB, one has to work on discipline, accuracy, pocket presence, and calmness under pressure. These things are examples of common causes that are inherent in one player.

Jim: That is a great illustration, Manju. Also, if I am correct, the description of these causes and their relation to variation came from Dr. Shewhart's contributions, correct?

Manju: You are quite right on that. The definition and further understanding of common or special cause variation came from Dr. Shewhart's work.

Dr. Shewhart pioneered the development of statistical process control (SPC) system to measure variation due to common and special causes. As I mentioned before, special cause variation occurs when something significant or special happens to the system (such as changes in weather conditions in QB example) and common cause variation occurs because of the inherent nature of the system. To improve common cause variation, significant system changes are necessary.

I will go into further details on both special and common cause variations later. For now, simply familiarize yourself with the general concept and the difference between the two.

Jim: Okay so Eat Healthy has five locations that are underperforming with only a 3.7% increase in sales. This number represents the actual performance, right?

Manju: Absolutely, that number represents actual performance. Suppose all five underperforming locations are located near each other and the data was collected just when a major storm hit the area. Suppose that a few weeks later, after the storm passes, the data was collected again, and we saw that the five underperforming locations had an increase in sales to 5%. Here, 3.7% is the actual performance under the special cause (major storm) and 5% is the capability. The target, however, is 7.5% increase in sales. To gain that 2.5% increase in sales to hit the goal, a number of changes at system level are required. If you remove special causes from your actual performance, you will reach your capability. If you have to reach your target from your capability, a lot of work needs to be done toward the overall system/process side. Now I will focus on phase 2 of data science approach. Phase 2 is related to analyzing the problem and collecting data.

Jim: Got it. Let's discuss phase 2.

3

Analyzing the Problem and Collecting Data

Game Plan: Deep Dive Analysis, Data Identification and Collection, and Understanding the Risk and Uncertainty

Manju: Let me now start the phase 2 of data science approach. Before you begin analyzing the data, you must first select the data. To do so, you must fundamentally understand your problem and begin selecting relevant data. With the abundance of data available today, it is important to ensure that the data you use for your project is clear, organized, and, most importantly, of good quality.

Jim: Manju, I guess here you will be touching upon the two important aspects of data "the right data" and "data should be right."

Manju: Exactly, Jim. It is absolutely important to understand what is the right data for the given problem and how that data correspond to your purpose. Now let us discuss "the deep dive analysis" part of this phase.

Deep Dive Analysis

Now that we have set a goal, we must begin choosing the information we believe is necessary to examine in order to solve our problem. Simply put, this step requires you to ask, "What are the core issues related to our problem." Suppose you are a mobile network provider and you want to figure out why customers are switching to a competing company, the core issues that a company may want to address include price, convenience, network quality, incentives, etc. These are called factors, variables, or drivers. In your case, Eat Healthy wants to understand why five locations are under-performing. Drivers they may want to examine could include population, ethnicity, price, desire to eat healthy food, coupons, etc. Understanding how and to what degree these factors affect sales will help begin the process of putting a plan in place to fix the issue.

Jim: So deep dive analysis is basically understanding and examining potential root cause drivers of the problem.

Manju: I think that's a good way to put it. Now let us focus on "data identification and collection."

Data Identification and Collection

Since data is viewed as a critical asset, many organizations have created a point person whose dedicated function is to manage data.

Jim: Manju, can you briefly explain data management in simple terms?

Manju: Sure, Jim. As data is being viewed as an important organizational asset, it is important to manage data efficiently and effectively. Data management should cover the two data aspects that we discussed earlier – "the right data" and "data should be right." For "the right data" part, the data management team should work with business people/data users to determine what data should be used/collected to solve the problem at hand. The other aspect "data should be right" is related to data quality, which we will discuss in detail.

The functions of data management can be broken down into four major constituents: data policy and governance, data strategy, data standards and data quality. To manage data, it is important to ensure that all constituents are coming together so that any data science project(s) undertaken by the organization has a good chance of being successful.

Jim: Manju, our firm is relatively small and we do not have a dedicated data management function. How should we handle data in those situations?

Manju: Good question, Jim. If you are a smaller business, it is important to assign someone within the organization with responsibility of managing data and in ensuring data management requirements are met. Does that make sense?

Jim: Absolutely.

Manju: Of all the functions of data management, I think data quality may be the single most important aspect of the data science process. Without good data, the results of your analysis could be flawed, rendering the changes you make futile. Data quality activities should include cleaning the data and ensuring the data is ready and fit-for-use for various decision-making activities.

> "Data! Data!" he cried impatiently, "I can't make bricks without clay."
> **–Conan Doyle-The Copper Beeches (Source: Rao, 1989)**

Jim: This is interesting. A lot of people talk about data quality when performing data-related activities. Although I nod my head when some people are talking about it, I actually don't understand the concept. Can you explain it?

Manju: Sure, Jim. Data quality activities can be considered as the process of detecting and correcting inaccurate data from the data sets. In my humble opinion, data should be corrected at its source level. Those who are leading data quality activities should focus on correcting data the first time at its source level. This will eliminate poor data going through subsequent stages of operations.

Jim: That sounds good. Can you give some examples in the context of Eat Healthy?

Manju: Certainly. Let's say in the case of your Eat Healthy example, customer location data is collected for some purpose by using US zip codes, which should have five digits. Here, if some values have less than or greater than five digits or do not correspond to codes for US customers, they are inaccurate and need to be changed or removed. Data quality analysis is also required if there are missing values for the zip code field for some customers.

Jim: Manju, this is all fine. Based on this discussion, can you explain the definition of good data?

Manju: Good data is data that is complete, valid, conforming to standards, and accurate. In addition, the hallmark of good data should be meeting customer needs, meaning it should be ready for the customers to receive desired insights. Unknown source, incomplete information, errors in reporting, etc. are all contributors to bad data. In larger organizations, the members of the data management team would check data quality and ensure that the underlying data is fit for the intended purpose. For smaller organizations, this process may be a little more laborious, as you would have to do it yourself.

Jim: Although labor-intensive, it might be good learning experience.

Manju: Absolutely. World-renowned statistician, Dr. C.R. Rao (Rao, 1989), provided a thorough checklist for vetting data, some of the questions he recommends asking are listed below.

C.R. Rao's Checklist
- How is data collected and recorded?
- Is the measurement system well defined?
- Is the data free from recording errors?
- Is the data from reliable sources and trustworthy?
- Are there any abnormalities or outliers associated with data?
- Is sample size adequate? Are all factors for data collection considered?
- Do you have the right kind of data that is suitable for the intended purpose?

Jim: This check list seems to cover all aspects of data quality. Very useful.

Manju: Yes, Jim. It does cover all aspects. For small businesses that don't have much of stored data, buying data or collecting data may be an additional step in the process. If you were to purchase data, ensuring that the company you buy it from is trustworthy will be essential. Purchasing industry standard data from a reliable data collections company would be a good way to begin your project and it will also ensure that the data is of good quality. If you are a small business looking to address a specific issue, collecting data yourself may be necessary. In this case, the person you have dedicated to hold the responsibilities of data management will need to ensure that the quality is satisfactory using the checklist provided above and through data quality analysis.

Jim: This sounds good. How do you actually measure data quality?

Manju: That is what I will be discussing now. Typically, data quality is measured for all metrics and associated variables in percentages based on four dimensions: completeness, conformity, validity, and accuracy. For example, if we were looking at a metric like income, we would need to measure the quality of data by assigning a percentage score for the four dimensions listed above. These percentages are called Data Quality scores (DQ scores).

Jim: Are DQ scores indicators of the data performance?

Manju: Absolutely. They are the indicators of data performance. Let me explain these four dimensions briefly. The completeness dimension ensures we have complete data to perform required analysis; the conformity ensures that data is available in required format; the validity ensures that data is presented with valid values; and accuracy ensures that the data is accurate and represents correctness of the data. The percentage scores then are simply the number of individual data points, which meet the requirements divided by the total.

Jim: Got it. Can you explain with examples?

Manju: Sure, Jim. So, suppose you have income data for 100 people in a certain area. If 93/100 cells are filled out, then your completeness score is 0.93 (or 93%). If 92/100 cells are in the correct format (for this example that would be dollars) then your conformity score is 0.92 (or 92%). Validity requires that you understand the meaning of the metric to ensure that the values are valid. So, for income having outliers that are likely mistakes will be important to notice. For example, having a data point read 50 million in an area where the average income is 50 thousand. Finally, accuracy refers to the verification of the data. It is important to ensure that a value given by someone is true. Using income data, looking at pay stubs/W2's to ensure people aren't inflating or deflating their income is important.

Jim: It's clear now with these examples. Sounds quite interesting. When you have all dimensional scores, how do you calculate the overall data quality score?

Manju: Excellent question. Let's say for income data, the dimensional scores are as follows: completeness: 0.93; conformity: 0.92; validity: 0.91; and accuracy: 0.9. Then, overall data quality score for income data is obtained by multiplying all the scores, which will be $0.93 \times 0.92 \times 0.91 \times 0.9$, which is equal to 0.70 (or 70%).

Jim, it is always good idea for a person conducting analysis to look at the data and confirm that is of good quality and ensure it is fit for the intended usage.

Jim: Okay, Manju. I know location manager of one of non-performing locations. I will contact him to help us with the data and then we can assess data quality.

Manju: That's awesome. Ask for sales increase numbers from the previous quarter and data on potential drivers such as ethnicity and discount/coupon information. If we get the data, we should be able assess the existing data quality.

Jim: Good news. I just got e-mail from the location manager. They can provide data files for the last quarter.

Manju: So quick! Then, let's meet after you get the data file and continue our discussion. We can meet in one week's time.

Jim: Sounds nice, Manju. I will have everything prepared for our next meeting.

Manju: See you soon, Jim.

(Jim gets data files from the location manager. He meets with Manju after one week to continue the discussion).

Jim: Hey, Manju. How are you? I have the data files.

Manju: I am fine, Jim. Let's look at the data files.

Jim: Okay.

Manju: Jim, by looking the data files, you can easily see some data quality issues. Some data is missing, and some is not valid. It is interesting to note that they have complete and accurate data at quarter level, which we used to create histograms.

Jim: Quarterly data is compiled by the sales and marketing team.

Manju: Do you think it is possible that the locations and marketing teams do not interact well enough to discuss data challenges/issues?

TABLE 3.1

Weekly Sales Numbers for Last Quarter

Week	# of Units Sold	% Increase in Sales
Previous week	2000	
WK1	2040	2
WK2	2101	2.99
WK3	2185	3.99
WK4		
WK5	2478	
WK6	2614	5.48
WK7	2718	3.97
WK8	2745	0.993
WK9	2766	0.765
WK10	2848	2.96
WK11	**29Y2** **(invalid)**	
WK12	3110	

Jim: That is quite possible.

Manju: That may be a topic for another discussion. For now, let us discuss the data quality issues in the weekly sales data (Table 3.1). If you look at the data corresponding to the number of units sold, we have missing data for week 4 and invalid entry for week 11, where a letter is present rather than a number. This will result in a completeness score of 92.30% ((12/13)×100)) and validity score of 84.61% ((11/13)×100). I think for weekly sales data, these two dimensions are relevant and sufficient. Using these two dimensions, the overall data quality score for # of units sold is the result of the multiplication of these two scores, which will be 78.10%. Because of these issues, data quality of % increase in sales is also affected as this quantity cannot be calculated for four weeks. So data quality score for this variable (% increase in sales) is 66.67% ((8/12)×100).

Jim: Thanks, Manju for this analysis. What about the next file? I think the next file has information on customers' ethnicity and information on discounts/coupons.

Manju: You are correct, Jim. The next file has this information (Table 3.2). This data also has some issues. If you look at Table 3.2, the completeness and validity scores for ethnicity are 84% and 80% with an overall data quality score of 67.2%. Similarly, the completeness

TABLE 3.2

Sample Data on Customers' Ethnicity and Discounts/Coupons

Customer	Ethnicity	Discounts/Coupons
1	White	No
2	**Mexican (invalid)**	Yes Invalid
3	White	**Yes/No (invalid)**
4	Asian	No
5	Asian	No
6		No
7	Asian	Yes
8	Asian	No
9	Asian	
10	Asian	No
11	Asian	Yes
12	African American	No
13		Yes
14	Hispanic	No
15	White	No
16	White	
17	Hispanic	Yes
18	White	Yes
19	Asian	**NA (invalid)**
20	Indian	No
21	Asian	No
22		
23		No
24	Asian	Yes
25	Asian	**Discount (invalid)**

and validity scores for coupons/discounts are 92% and 80% with overall data quality score of 73.6%. Similar to the case prior, the dimensions completeness and validity are relevant and sufficient here as well.

Jim: Thanks, Manju. I will send this information to the location manager and ask him to look into this.

Manju: Sounds good.

Jim: I just heard from the location manager. They can look into sales data and correct it. For the other data file, they need more time. I asked them to send the corrected sales data file once it is fixed.

Manju: Great. Then, we can look at the correct numbers for sales at least.

> Figures won't lie, but liars will figure.
> **– General Charles H. Grosvenor**
> **(Source: Rao, 1989)**

As you might realize now, people often take data quality for granted and end up using bad data to conduct analysis. This bad data can lead people to the answers they desire but may not be reflective of the truth.

Jim: You're saying we can get the answers we want to hear and not necessarily the answers that will help our business.

Manju: Exactly. You can only address a problem if you know what the problem actually is. Good data helps ensure that you get down to the root cause. Since Eat Healthy is a smaller chain with a small data management function, for them acquiring the data and ensuring that it is of good quality is not as difficult. Of course, they will also need to choose drivers to further analyze, such as population, ethnicity, average household income, desire to eat healthy, and discounts/coupons.
Also, while, running a project, it is impossible to fully foresee every potential hiccup, so all of this comes with a fair amount of risk.

Jim: What types of risk should we be aware of?

Manju: Risk and uncertainty concepts have been in existence for a long time. We come across uncertainties and face their effects from time to time in the environment we live. Most of us hope for things to happen as expected, but in reality things will be different. Risk and uncertainty exist everywhere, including the world of data science.

So, now let me explain how we can understand the risk and uncertainty and take actions to mitigate them.

Understanding the Risk and Uncertainty

Jim: Manju, once we understand the risk and uncertainty and take actions, will the problems due to risk be eliminated?

Manju: No, Jim. There are ways to understand the risk and uncertainty and mitigate them within a project but there is no way to fully eliminate them. Risk and uncertainty are intrinsically a part of life and business. The purpose of this section is to breakdown what I consider to be the six core sources of risk and uncertainty you may encounter in your data science project.

> If we don't know, we cannot act
> If we cannot act, the risk of loss is high
> If we do know and act, the risk can be managed
> If we do know and fail to act, we deserve the loss
> **– Mikel J Harry, Co-creator and Principle Architect of Six Sigma**

The Six Core Sources of Risk and uncertainty:
1. Risk and uncertainty in data measurement errors
2. Risk and uncertainty due to the existence of variation
3. Risk and uncertainty in prediction, diagnosis and decision-making
4. Risk and uncertainty in analytics process execution
5. Risk and uncertainty due to incomplete information
6. Risk and uncertainty due to procrastination

Depending on the size of your business, some of these sources of risk may be more/less applicable than others. It is important to be aware of any and all sources of risk in order to avoid issues in your project.

Jim: Manju, I agree that the first five are related to data science in one way or other. I am just not sure how the last one is related.

Manju: This is something that is quite important in my opinion. In the context of data science, it is related to delayed decisions or actions based on analytical findings. It's more on execution and deployment of analytics findings.

Jim: Got it.

Manju: Now, let's dive into the first source of risk and uncertainty related to data measurement errors.

Risk and Uncertainty in Data Measurement Error

Accurate and appropriate measurements are essential to a good data science project. If we do not measure the correct things, we are at a risk of working on the wrong initiatives yielding inaccurate results. Measurement comes down to two basic things: what to measure and how to measure it. "What to measure" requires an understanding of the problem at hand and what drivers will be examined in order to address the issue. "How to measure" is about setting organizational standards that ensure that anybody who takes measurements or reads measurements and records them as data points does so in a consistent (standard) way. It is important to make sure that the data is uniform in its collection and representation.

Jim: Manju, wait a second. I think here you are touching upon two aspects of data, right? I think what to measure correspond to "the right data" aspect.

Manju: Absolutely Jim. You are correct. "What to measure "correspond to "the right data" aspect. However, the "how to measure part" is an important requirement for the "data should be right" aspect. The "data should be right" aspect should also include the other dimensions of data quality that we discussed earlier.

Jim: Got it. The "how to measure" part deals with the way data is collected, suitable measurement instruments, their accuracy, etc. Am I correct?

Manju: You are correct on this. If Eat Healthy was looking to see how far, on average, a customer has to travel to come to their restaurant and it was not specified whether they wanted the value in miles, kilometers, blocks, minutes, etc., then they may have major errors in the data. For example, the number 6 in a value field could be associated with anything, that is, 6 minutes, 6 miles, 6 blocks, etc. Errors in these situations often occur due to poor definitions and concepts, bias in the measurements and differences in the measurement instruments and investigators. Once you address your data quality, it is important to associate a certain degree of confidence to the measurements. In other words, we should ascertain how confident we are with our quality of measurements.

Jim: Can you talk more about degree of confidence?

Manju: Sure, Jim, the degree of confidence is a measure of probability. It is a way to quantify uncertainty. We can provide a lower bound and upper bound to the measured values with 90% or 95% or 99% confidence. This way we can provide an estimate to the trustworthiness of the information. As an example, we can say with 95% confidence (probability) that on an average, a customer waits between ten and fifteen minutes to get their food at Eat Healthy. In the case of data quality estimates also, we can use confidence levels to ascertain degree of confidence. For example, with 95% confidence, we can say that the data quality of "travel distance "is 85%. Confidence level is a degree with which we can believe the estimates of parameters to be accurate. Confidence level-based estimates are calculated based on a statistical estimation theory in which we use sample data under specific degrees of confidence (90%, 95% or 99%).

Jim: I assume software programs can be easily used to obtain estimates based on different confidence levels, right? This concept is very interesting. However, if we have to use complicated formulas to calculate the estimates, then it will be tough.

Manju: Several statistical packages/programs provide estimates for confidence levels very easily for the given data sets. So, you don't have to worry about complicated formulas. In fact, to be honest, many high-school courses teach students these concepts and their applicability, which goes to show how easy they are to understand.

Jim: Wow! I kind of feel stupid after asking that question.

Manju: There is no such thing as a stupid question Jim. All questions are important. Coming back to our topic, we can also set confidence levels for measurements such as defect rate. A defect for Eat Healthy can be a person waiting for the food longer than the expected window or range. In that case, the defect rate is the percentage of people who are waiting for more than the specified range. So, for Eat Healthy, we could say with 99% confidence that only 3%–8% of the customers will wait longer than the given window.

Jim: Got it, Manju.

Manju: Now let's discuss second type of risk on our list.

Risk and Uncertainty Due to the Existence of Variation

We discussed briefly about variation, when we were formulating the problem in one of our first meetings.

Jim: Yes. I remember that. You explained standard deviation, a measure of variation and talked about the concept of statistical control.

Manju: Yes. Good memory. Let us go into the details of this topic now. I will use the same figure (for % sales increase in performing locations) that we used earlier. For a better understanding of the topic, I am using the same figure here (Figure 3.1).

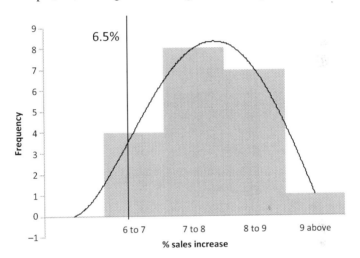

FIGURE 3.1
Description of variation with performing locations data.

Jim: Okay. Sounds good.

Manju: In this figure, let us say that any value less than 6.5% is not acceptable for performing locations. In other words, this value represents target performance. Any deviation from the target (less than 6.5% in this case) is undesirable and this is called variation. In quality terms, variation is considered as enemy of performance quality. Any deviation from performance quality (including individual's performance in the context of daily routine, such as workout and eating habits) is undesirable and needs to be corrected.

Jim: Makes lot of sense. Usually when I track health indicators using my mobile device, I am actually looking at anomalies due to variation. I agree it's very important.

Manju: That's great, Jim. Note that in case of variables like strength and weight, the deviation can happen if the values deviate on either side from the target. For example, if the target weight is 150 pounds, anything less or greater than this number will cause variation.

Jim: Got it. In weight example, there will be issues with underweight and overweight.

Manju: You got it. Understanding the sources of variation, so that we can act upon them and make the observation and measurement as consistent as possible and close to the target, will help greatly in mitigating any associated risk due to variation. The sources of variation can come from a range of factors such as methods, feeds, humans, measurements, etc. as shown in Figure 3.2. Figure 3.2 is a typical process representation with inputs, outputs, and sources of variation. In a given process/system, these factors will have different effects. Variation risk mitigation requires a detailed understanding of the process and associated factors that cause variation.

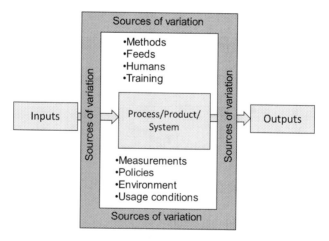

FIGURE 3.2
Sources of variation.

Jim: The concept of variation is interesting. What is a good way to monitor variation?

Manju: Great question, Jim. Statistical Process Control (SPC) is an effective method to monitor variation and understand the extent of variation. SPC is a data-driven method for measuring consistency and ensuring the predictability of the processes. This concept was first introduced by Walter Shewhart in the first half of the twentieth century. Controlling a process makes it more predictable by reducing process variability and clearly distinguishing the causes of variation (common causes and special causes). The aim of SPC is to understand the variation associated with processes.

A primary tool for SPC is the control chart; a time series plot that represents the set of measurements, along with their mean, upper control limit, and lower control limit (UCL and LCL). These limits are three standard deviations (σ) from the mean of the measurements.

Jim: Oh. Yes. I recall our discussion about histogram and standard deviation earlier when you talked about determining outliers using three standard deviation limits.

Manju: Yes, Jim. I used the same logic there. So, the SPC charts help detect points of unusual or unexpected variation (i.e., measurements above the UCL or below the LCL). Figure 3.3 shows various components of a control chart. The control chart illustrates the stability, predictability, and capability of the process with a visual display of variation. If the measurements are between the LCL and UCL, we can say the measurements are stable and predictable, in other words they are in control and this variation is expected. The distance between the LCL and UCL indicates the consistency of measurements. Smaller distance means better consistency and higher capability, and vice versa.

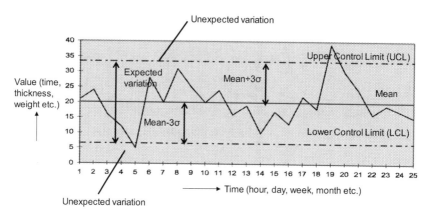

FIGURE 3.3
Control chart and its components.

Jim: Manju, how do you calculate control limits to monitor the process/
system performance?

Manju: Typically, we use past or historical data for building control limits
and use those limits for future monitoring and control. Through
the historical data one can calculate the mean or average and
the standard deviation (σ). The control limits are placed at three
times standard deviations from the mean. So, the average minus
three standard deviations will give us the LCL and the average
plus three times standard deviations will give us the UCL.

Jim: Manju, why should we take three standard deviations on either side
of the mean?

Manju: Very important question. If we take three standard deviation on
either side of mean, probabilistically 99.73% similar observations lie within LCL and UCL. The observations that are not in
the range of LCL and UCL are outliers due to some special cause
variation. Most statistical programs will calculate and set the LCL
and UCL for you. This is just a brief explanation of what it means.

Jim: This is excellent, Manju. What should we do when we don't have historical data?

Manju: Another good question. When historical data is not there, you
need to start collecting data on that process/system. Once you
have sufficient data, you can build control limits to control the
process/system.

Jim: Got it.

TABLE 3.3

# of Errors per Week

Week	# of Errors
WK1	4
WK2	7
WK3	5
WK4	2
WK5	8
WK6	12
WK7	2
WK8	4
WK9	5
WK10	2
WK11	4
WK12	5

Manju: In fact, if you have some data, I can show how to construct a control chart and what interpretations we can make from it.

Jim: I do have some data that I can share. This is the data for the number of errors in 100 units at an Eat Healthy location while serving plant-based food in the last quarter. The same location provided us sales data and data on other variables. Here is the data in Table 3.3.

Manju: Awesome! For this data, let us calculate the average, standard deviation, and control limits. By the way, did you receive the corrected data file for sales data from this location.

Jim: Let me check my messages. Yes. I did receive the updated sales data. The details are in Table 3.4.

Manju: Great. With this data, we can see if there is a correlation between number of errors and sales numbers.

Jim: Manju, I am very curious to see the results.

Manju: Sure, Jim. Let me calculate the required quantities from this data. For the number of errors (data in Table 3.3), the average is 5 and the standard deviation is 2.2. So, UCL will be $5+3\times2.2=11.6$ and LCL is $5-3\times2.2=-1.6$. In an example like this, we can't have negative errors; so, the LCL is set to zero. I will construct the control chart for this data, it will be as shown in Figure 3.4.

TABLE 3.4

Weekly Sales Numbers for Last Quarter (Corrected Data)

Week	# of Units Sold	% Increase in Sales
Previous week	2000	
WK1	2040	2
WK2	2101	2.99
WK3	2185	3.99
WK4	2338	7
WK5	2478	5.98
WK6	2614	5.48
WK7	2718	3.97
WK8	2745	0.993
WK9	2766	0.765
WK10	2848	2.96
WK11	2962	4
WK12	3110	4.99

(Manju takes few minutes to construct the control chart as shown in Figure 3.4 and the simple time-series chart for % increase in sales data as shown in Figure 3.5.)

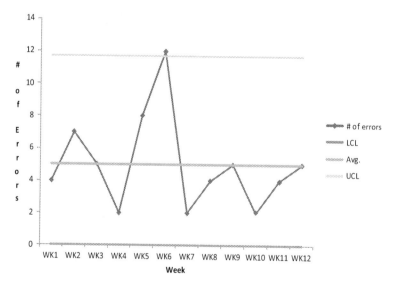

FIGURE 3.4

Control chart for # of errors.

Manju: If you look at the control chart, by and large most of the errors are lower than the UCL. Week 6 was the highest and above the UCL. Week 5 also shows a somewhat higher error rate. These spikes must be due to special causes.

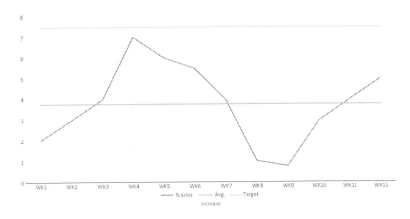

FIGURE 3.5
% increase in weekly sales (target is 7.5%).

Jim: Yes. I see that.

Manju: If we look at the sales data in Table 3.4 and Figure 3.5, the average % sales increase is 3.75%. Weeks 8 and 9 have very low sales increase percentages. I am suspecting that high error rates during weeks 5 and 6 have impacted the sales numbers in subsequent weeks as customers might not be happy and did not return. Jim, did anything special happened during weeks 5 and 6?

Jim: These two weeks are first two weeks in May. Oh, yes! During these two weeks, we hired new people in that location. They were probably not fully accustomed to the system. I can dig deeper into it by talking to the location manager.

Manju: You see you already identified some possible special causes. That is the power of the control chart. Also, Jim, remember these control limits are typically used for future control and they need to be periodically updated with the most recent data.

Jim: Fascinating, Manju. I can definitely see the value of a control chart and how it helps in understanding variation. Through this approach, we can measure and monitor the performance of a metric.

Manju: I completely agree. In this context, let me quickly explain the three aspects of a metric: Actual, Capability, and Target for the sales data. We discussed these aspects earlier. For % increase in sales for the data in Table 3.4, the Actual performance is average sales, which is 3.75%. If we discard weeks 8 and 9 (special cause variation), then the average is 4.34%, which is the Capability. As we know the Target is 7.5%.

Jim: Absolutely. Makes sense.

Manju: Do you have any questions, Jim?

Jim: Does the control chart approach apply to machine learning (ML) and artificial intelligence (AI)?

Manju: Great question. Machine learning is a branch of artificial intelligence (AI) through which a system's ability will be enhanced from historical data and experience. The subject of AI deals with providing intelligence to systems so that they automatically perform all operations. I think, in the case of a control chart we are doing something similar at a very rudimentary level. We take historical data in order to calculate control limits, and they are then used for future control and monitoring. If we automate this approach, the systems can periodically take the most recent data and modify control limits as needed for future controls. In other words, we can monitor performance based on historical data through automation.

Jim: I think it makes sense, Manju. Are we done discussing risk and uncertainty due to variation?

Manju: Yes, Jim. Now let us discuss the third type of risk and uncertainty that is related to prediction, diagnosis, and decision-making.

Risk and Uncertainty in Prediction, Diagnosis, and Decision-Making

Risk and uncertainty in prediction, diagnosis and decision-making deals with errors associated with the variables used in the models. Usually, we denote the variable to be determined as Y (dependent variable) and variables impacting Y as X1, X2, X3... (independent variables) and use the following functional relation to describe this:

Y = f (X1, X2, X3....)

The above relation is read as Y is a function of the variables X1, X2, X3...

Jim: You are saying that Y can be controlled by controlling X's. Sometimes, it is possible that we might not be able to control some X's though they impact Y. Am I making sense?

Manju: Absolutely, Jim. Not every X can be controlled. The X's that we can control are called control factors and X's that we cannot control are called uncontrollable or noise factors. For example, if the variable that needs to be determined, Y is wait time in minutes at a restaurant then X's can be number of tables, location, time/day of week etc. Understanding these factors/variables is important to determine or have some knowledge about the wait time. These factors can be controlled and so they are usually called control factors. The variation in Y can occur due to these factors. Variation in Y can also occur due to other factors that cannot be controlled such as power outage, weather conditions, and traffic (due to which restaurant staff does not show up on time) . So, these factors are called uncontrollable factors or noise factors. The variation due to noise factors should be reduced as much as possible with suitable mitigation strategies. This is what is done in Taguchi's robust design approach.

Jim: I have heard about Taguchi. His methods are popular worldwide, right?

Manju: True, Jim. Dr. Taguchi, a great Japanese engineer, did a lot of work in the area of robust design. He effectively applied statistics in many industrial applications and contributed immensely to the field of quality engineering. His methods have been applied across the globe and companies saved millions of dollars because of them.

Taguchi came up with the idea of robust design. Robust design aims at providing consistent performance of products, systems, and even models by minimizing the effect of uncontrollable/noise factors. Adequate knowledge about uncontrollable or noise factors is also very important to make the design robust. Taguchi further recommends testing a product or system or model performance under extreme noise conditions, so that they produce robust performance in all conditions.

Jim: Got it. I think "robust" in the context of Taguchi means making the product/system insensitive to noise factors, so the product/system performs in the same manner always.

Manju: You are correct, Jim. By making your product/system insensitive to noise factors, you are taking action toward risk due to noise factor variation. In addition, we need to have a plan to handle variation due to controllable factors. So for this type of variation-related risk, the mitigation plan should be to understand the functional relationship between the dependent variable to be determined (Y) and independent factors (X1, X2...) and have adequate knowledge about these factors so suitable actions can be taken. Note that the X1, X2... can be control factors and noise factors.

Jim: Understood.

Manju: In my opinion, sometimes predictions fail because of lack of understanding of noise factors and their effects when they are at extreme (adverse) conditions. If we had a good understanding of the noise factors and associated extreme conditions and took prompt actions against them, events such as the 9/11 attacks and the coronavirus pandemic, their adverse effects could have been prevented or minimized. No one seriously considered a terrorist attack could happen using commercial planes. Subsequently, the governments under various regimes became more knowledgeable and more proactive to prevent major attacks on US soil.

Jim: I think similar conclusions can also be drawn with regard to the failure to foresee a pandemic such as the Coronavirus.

Manju: Absolutely. If we had foreseen this and taken prompt actions, things would have been much better. Now let's move on to other type of risk and uncertainty, related to analytics process execution.

Risk and Uncertainty in Analytics Process Execution

Let's say we are trying to evaluate the taste of Eat Healthy's plant-based burgers based on several factors and the management wants to do this using analytics. For this purpose, the management needs to come up with a suitable analytical model that should be part of a sound analytics execution process. In my opinion, most often we perform analytics without having a good approach for execution. I think this is a big mistake. When you have a sound approach, during analytics execution, we should be able to understand risk associated with various process elements.

Jim: Okay. How exactly are we going to do that?

Manju: Let's take the same example of taste evaluation of plant-based burgers. To do this, the Eat Healthy management needs to know what kinds of risk they can foresee while executing analytical operations to come up with a model for evaluating taste. They may have process elements as shown in Figure 3.6. The trick here is to understand and score the probability of the occurrence of issues/problems related to process elements. Scoring can be done using a scale between 1 and 7 with 1 indicating that problem/issue due to process element is very unlikely and 7 indicating it is very likely.

Jim: I am guessing we also need to score severity part-right?

Manju: True. we also need to understand and score the severity of issues/problems related to process elements. Again, scoring can be done using a scale between 1 and 7 with 1 indicating that problem/issue is negligible and 7 indicating that the problem/issue is critical. Then, we multiply these two scores to get risk factor (RF). RF is used to prioritize issues due to process elements. This will help us take proper action to mitigate associated risk. So how do we get these scores? The scores are based on discussions where teams of subject matter experts will gather, brainstorm, and do the scoring.

Jim: Some time ago I was trained on failure mode analysis. They used something similar to RF to quantify risk due to factors.

Manju: This type of approach is used frequently in process improvement projects to quantify and prioritize project risks.

Now let's see what we can infer from the risk assessment matrix in Figure 3.6. It is clear that "defining metrics" and "data quality" have the highest RF values and so they are classified as "very high" risk process elements that need to be addressed first, followed by data acquisition which is classified as "high" risk process element and so on.

Jim: This is a very good way to list and prioritize various risks so we can work on critical issues first. What is next, Manju?

Risk Assessment Matrix		Risk Evaluation					
Process Element	Prob. of occ	Score	Severity	Score	Risk Factor (RF)	Risk Prioritization
Defining metrics	Very likely	7	Critical	7	49	Very high
Data acquisiion	Likely	5	Critical	7	35	High
Data quality	Very likely	7	Critical	7	49	Very high
Availability of suitable tools	Unlikely	3	Critical	7	21	Moderate
Technology dependence	Very unlikely	1	Marginal	3	3	Low

Prob. of occ.: 1-Very unlikely; 3-Unlikely; 5-Likely; 7-Very likely

Severity: 1-Negligible; 3-Marginal; 5-Significant; 7-Critical

FIGURE 3.6
Risk assessment matrix.

Manju: Now let's focus on risk and uncertainty due to incomplete information.

Jim: Sounds nice.

Risk and Uncertainty Due to Incomplete Information

Manju: Jim, I just want to clarify that this type of risk is not related to incomplete data that we discussed as part of data quality issues earlier.

Jim: Okay. What does this type of risk relate to?

Manju: This relates to statistical risk related to samples and risk of not knowing what technique/model to use for the problem at hand.

Jim: Got it.

Manju: Risk and uncertainty due to incomplete information can be discussed in two scenarios. One is statistical risk with inadequate or bad samples and second is risk of not knowing something.

Let us discuss first part – statistical risk. We usually take sample data to make inferences about the entire population, which is what we do with inferential statistics. When you do not represent the population with a good sample, it will give wrong results and therefore it affects decision-making.

Jim: Manju, what is a good sample?

Manju: According to me, good sample provides data to draw credible inferences with a high degree of confidence that can be acted upon. So, this sampling aspect is quite important, and it must be taken into account while performing data analysis. Usually, there are techniques like rational sampling that are used to select unbiased samples to represent populations.

Jim: If we have good unbiased sample then we can mitigate issues related to sampling. Got it.

Manju: Good. Now let us briefly discuss risk of not knowing what technique/model to use.

Jim: Looking forward to it.

Manju: After selecting the sample, there is a possibility for other risks such as what model/technique needs to be used for the problem at hand? Clear problem definition will help us ask right questions. To answer the right questions, we need to select a suitable model/technique. Otherwise, there is a risk of providing wrong answers and that will end up resulting in a bad decision. Many times, when we have so much data, it is a natural tendency to use a software package to run analysis without knowing if that analysis would provide the correct answers. Sometimes people also perform analysis without knowing who are the users of such analysis. Such things happen quite a lot. So, it is absolutely important to select a suitable model/technique to perform required analysis and provide the right answers. In addition, one also should know who will be using such results. The risk of not knowing can cause tremendous damage. For example, it can prevent us from knowing whether any abnormalities are potentially dangerous or not. Knowing about them allows us to decide whether or not we need to address them.

Jim: Lot of times we take many things for granted and act without knowing fully about them. These actions will result in bad outcomes and might incur huge losses.

Manju: Well said. Now let's discuss the last type of risk which is due to procrastination.

Risk and Uncertainty Due to Procrastination

As I mentioned earlier, this is something that is quite important in my opinion. In the context of a data science, delayed decisions or actions based on analytical findings will cause tremendous damage because of two reasons-(1) the problem will continue to exist and (2) you are wasting all the effort (time, resources, money, etc.) that was put in for problem solving. This will also affect the morale of the people who worked on the effort.

Jim: Agreed. This happened quite a lot in my work life although not related to analytical decisions.

Manju: Yes, Jim. These things happen. They can occur in industry or in government, when leaders fail to act on certain things immediately. Knowing is not enough. In order to ensure results, you must act.

Jim: Well said, Manju. It was a great discussion about risk and uncertainty. Now, please tell me what types of risks do you think are applicable to Eat Healthy?

Manju: For Eat Healthy, I think the most applicable risks are:

1. Risk and uncertainty in data measurement errors;
2. Risk and uncertainty due to existence of variation;
3. Risk and uncertainty in prediction, diagnosis, and decision-making.

To handle the first risk you need to ensure that measurement systems are accurate and reliable. The data errors should be corrected at the source levels so that you will be confident about the data to be analyzed. We already addressed this using your data files. For risk due to existence of variation, you may want to use the control chart approach and analyze patterns associated with sales corresponding to non-performing locations We addressed this as well using control chart analysis. For risk and uncertainty in prediction, diagnosis, and decision-making, you may want to ensure that errors corresponding to relevant variables (controllable and noise) are taken into consideration.

Jim: Thanks, Manju for this explanation. This is very clear.

Manju: No problem. So, risk and uncertainty management is quite important. Risk and uncertainty cause variation in product performance and analytical results, which will adversely impact the decision-making activities. Here, I would like to highlight the importance of the loss function. Through the loss function concept, Genichi Taguchi established a relationship between variation and loss to society.

Jim: Interesting. I am curious to learn about the loss function concept.

Manju: According to loss function, if product performance and analytical results deviate from the target there is a loss. This loss can be in the form of product failures, customer dissatisfaction, company bankruptcies, loss of reputation, etc. The loss increases if there is deviation on either side of the target (m) as shown in Figure 3.7. In this Figure, Y represents a metric corresponding to the product performance or analytical result, and $L(Y)$ is the loss to society. Here "society" includes customers, organizations, government, etc. When Y is equal to m, the target value, the loss is zero. Please note that what you are seeing in Figure 3.7 is the ideal loss function, which is symmetrical. In practice, the loss function will not be completely symmetrical since calculations are based on estimations.

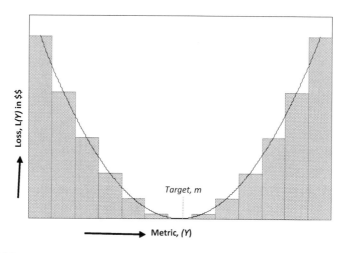

FIGURE 3.7
Taguchi's loss function.

Jim: Manju, I have a question. For the metric like ours, % sales increase, how will you use the loss function?

Manju: Awesome question, Jim. In those situations, only one half of the loss function is applicable. There will be loss only if the % sales increase is less than the target value. If it is higher than the target, that is a good situation since you want higher sales numbers. In the case of Eat Healthy for % sales increase, if the target value is 7.5% then anything less than 7.5% will cause deviation and hence loss and so, only the left side of the loss function (Figure 3.5) is applicable. Similarly, there are situations where the right side of the loss function is applicable. If your metric is defect rate, anything lower than the target is desirable and anything higher than the target is undesirable, and, therefore, the right side of loss function is applicable.

Jim: Thanks, Manju! Wow. This is an eye opener. Through loss function, everyone can understand about the importance of deviation (variation) from the target and its impact to society. In the case of Eat Healthy, for non-performing locations, I think we can say that loss could come from the deviation from the overall performance and it can be related to factors such as not understanding customer preferences, poor taste, etc., right?

Manju: Absolutely. I am glad you are trying to connect your firm's situation to these ideas.

Jim: Yes. That is important. That is how one can learn better.

Manju: I agree. Now let's start phase 3 of our overall approach, Creating and Analyzing Models.

Jim: I am ready for that.

4

Creating and Analyzing Models

PHASE 3

Game Plan: Data Analysis, Model Selection, and Outcome Analysis

Manju: Let me now discuss the phase 3 of data science approach.

Data Analysis and Model Selection
Data analytics should provide insights to address our core problem as well as provide a direction to help in future activities (Rao, 1989). So, data analytics should have a clear purpose.

> Scientific laws are not advanced by the principle of authority or justified by faith or medieval philosophy; statistics is the only court of appeal to new knowledge.
> **–P.C. Mahalanobis, Founder of Indian Statistical Institute (Source: Rao, 1989)**

Jim: I think a clear definition of the problem and the goal statement will provide that purpose and based on that one can choose a suitable analytical method or technique, right?

Manju: That's right. The purpose can be for business, government, or educational problems. Just loading data into a software program and performing analysis with some techniques would not provide the solution that we need if you do not have clear purpose. Once the purpose is clearly articulated, we can perform analytics successfully. Successful analytics are usually simple to use, accurate, precise, and scaled quickly.

Jim: Are you saying that these are important characteristics of analytics?

Manju: Yes. In my view, analytics should have the characteristics listed above. Let me summarize those for you.

DOI: 10.4324/9781003165279-4

Characteristics of Successful Analytics

- Simple to use and explain
- Should be able to scale quickly
- Should be accurate and precise

Jim: I understand these characteristics. I have a question now. What types of analytics are out there and how do we choose the right ones for our specific needs?

Manju: Very relevant question. Luckily, most of the analytics that we run are based on techniques that have already been developed. Usually, all we need to do is select a technique/model that is best suited for a given data set. In Figure 4.1, we have an illustration of various types of analytics derived to address specific purposes. This includes the types that Gartner (2012) proposed.

Jim: Interesting. Can you explain the different types of analytics a little more?

Manju: Sure! Below, I am providing descriptions of various types of analytics.

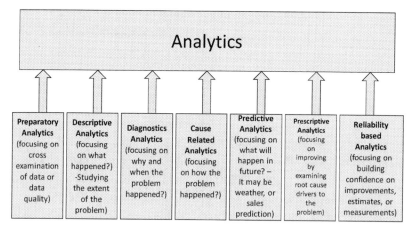

FIGURE 4.1
Different types of analytics.

Different Types of Analytics

> **Preparatory analytics:** The purpose of preparatory analytics is to conduct a cross-examination of the data to ensure data quality. Ideally, we need to ensure data quality at the time of data collection. In other words, data quality should be built into the system while collecting the data.

Jim: Let me stop you here. I recall our discussion on two important aspects of data quality – "the right data" and "data should be right". Once we identify the right data, then preparatory analytics is to ensure the second aspect "data should be right". Is my thinking correct here?

Manju: Absolutely. You nailed it quite well. Once we ensure that the data is right, we can use the other types of analytics. Let me describe those now.

> **Descriptive analytics:** Descriptive analytics deals with answering questions like what happened to the performance of a particular metric, system, process, or product. Graphical techniques such as histograms and bar graphs and stability, and capability analysis using descriptive statistics are quite useful in this type of analytics.

> **Diagnostic analytics:** This type of analytics is useful to understand when, where, why and how a particular problem has occurred. Typical tools and techniques used in this type of analytics are correlation analysis, hypothesis tests, and control charts.

> **Cause-related analytics:** Cause-related analytics are intended to conduct root cause analysis for understanding causes of the problems or failures. Techniques like cause and effect diagrams and a cause and effect matrix are quite useful for this type of analytics.

> **Predictive analytics:** If the goal is to predict the behavioral patterns associated with a process, product, or system, predictive analytics are used. Techniques like artificial neural networks and regression analysis are useful to perform predictive analytics.

> **Prescriptive analytics:** Prescriptive analytics are useful in answering questions like how we can improve performance. Techniques like experimental design are used in prescriptive analytics.

Reliability-based analytics: To estimate the reliability of a product, process, systems, or set of models with a required degree of confidence, we use this type of analytics. Failure analysis, confidence intervals, signal-to-noise ratios, etc. are quite useful in this type of analytics.

Jim: Good to see these groupings. I think it's important to classify reliability-based analytics in a separate group. For the first time I am seeing this type of grouping. Very interesting.

Manju: Jim, I am glad you noticed that. Also, most software programs are equipped with tools for the analytics that I have mentioned. So, one need not get too intimidated.

Jim: This helps a lot, Manju. Thank you so much. I guess in our daily activities we are also using and making plans based on some of these types of analytics. For example, weather predictions are made based on predictive analytics and we use this information to plan activities, trips, etc.

Manju: Exactly, Jim. Nowadays, everybody is using data-based information to prepare for daily activities. Essentially, we select a type or types of analytics and use them to begin addressing our problems. Regardless of the type(s) of analytics you choose, the insights from them will be deployed in decision-making activities and are also useful in providing a direction for future activities.

Jim, based on different types of analytics we discussed, what type/types of analytics will be useful for solving the Eat Healthy's problem that we are dealing with?

Jim: I think Eat Healthy will probably use the preparatory, descriptive, diagnostic, and predictive models.

Manju: You got it, Jim. I think they are the right types of analytics to use in Eat Healthy's case.

Jim: So interesting. Now that we have picked a model, what is the process of analytics execution within an organization?

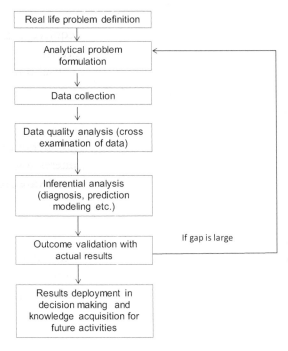

FIGURE 4.2
Problem formulation and analytics execution.

Manju: That is what I will be explaining now. Please refer to Figure 4.2. I would like to emphasize three things in the figure above. First, the importance of data quality (DQ) or cross-examination of data (step 4). In my opinion, typically most analysts miss this step and this is where the analytics can fail. The second thing that I want to highlight is step 6: validate the output with the actual outcomes. This is extremely important to evaluate model quality. Model outputs must be as close to the actual outcomes as possible. If the gap between these two is large, then we need to go back to step 2: the formulation step. The third thing is the most important for execution of analytics: senior management support. Without the support and commitment of senior management in an organization, most projects will fail.

Jim: Got it! By the way, what do you mean by inferential analysis in Figure 4.2? Can you elaborate?

> Life is the art of drawing sufficient conclusions from insufficient premises.
>
> **–Samuel Butler (Source: Rao, 1989)**

Manju: Of course, Jim. In using inferential analysis, we will basically try to infer or predict the performance or extent of variability within a product or system by analyzing sample data. We use sample data to infer about large populations. Since we use samples with limited information, it is important for us to select those samples accurately. In my opinion, all types of analytics that we discussed are part of inferential analysis.

Jim: So inferential analysis means, looking at sample data and understanding what it is telling you regarding the entire population.

Manju: That's it.

Jim: Okay.

Manju: Now, I personally feel there should be one added step to Figure 4.2. That step is to measure how effective your analytics execution is. To measure the quality of analytics execution, one can use the robust quality index (RQI).

> RQI (Jugulum, 2019) is a holistic quality measure that includes data quality and analytics accuracy. This comprehensive index takes into account both data quality aspects and analytical aspects so that one can measure the overall quality of analytics execution from start to finish. RQI is measured on a scale of 0–100, the higher number indicates better quality. It can also be used to evaluate the effectiveness of artificial intelligence (AI) and machine learning (ML) models, as they are also fundamentally analytical approaches.

Jim: Interesting. Tell me more about this.

Manju: For example, let us say Eat Healthy is trying to predict the quality of plant-based burger through three variables: plant-based patty, condiment (ketchup, mustard, etc.), and bun. After collecting data on those variables, their DQ is calculated based on completeness and validity dimensions. The following Table 4.1 shows the details of these DQ calculations.

TABLE 4.1

Data Quality (DQ) Scores

	DQ Dimensional Scores (%)		
Variable	**Completeness**	**Validity**	**DQ Score**
Plant-based patty	96	94.5	91
Condiment (ketchup, mustard, etc.)	95	91.5	87
Bun	92	92.4	85

TABLE 4.2

Robust Quality Index (RQI) Calculation

Variable	**Scores**	**Target**	
Plant-based patty	91	95	
Condiment (ketchup, mustard, etc.)	87	90	
Bun	85	90	
Burger taste/Model output	7.5	10	
		RQI for Analytics	43

Jim: Alright. This is DQ component. I think now you will bring in analytical component, right?

Manju: You got it, Jim. Let us say that they built a model to calculate a value for taste. The taste is measured on a scale of 1–10 with 10 being best. Using this, the plant-based burger taste value was calculated, and the value was 7.5. Based on data quality and analytics quality, RQI was evaluated and it was equal to 43. Table 4.2 shows details of the RQI calculation. Just FYI, RQI is based on mean-squared deviations and signal-to-noise ratios. I can provide details about these calculations if you want.

Jim: Ok, this is very good. I would love to get the details about these calculations. Also, can we dive a little deeper into what this means? Looking at the overall quality of 43, can we say that there is a lot of room for improvement?

Manju: You are correct, Jim. There is a lot of room for improvement since 43 is somewhere closer to middle on the scale for which the maximum value is 100.

Jim: Understood. Manju, earlier we briefly addressed that a data analytics software program would be necessary to solve data science problems. Would you want to expand on that?

Manju: Absolutely, Jim. In addition to analytics software programs, we also need some tech. expertise. I will now want to briefly discuss on the tech expertise and software programs required.

Jim: I am ready for this discussion now.

Manju: As far as tech expertise is concerned, we need to extract the data from different systems by writing simple queries and we need to understand the data files as well. For these things, technology groups help can be taken. In addition, we should be very comfortable with commonly used data programs like Excel and comma separated values (csv) to store and use the data. These formats are very commonly used in lot of applications and people can grasp them very easily. Usually in companies, the chief data officer or someone with a similar function can take care of training people to extract data and run software programs. It is also possible that just through the use of excel and csv programs, many data requirements can be met and one can run data-related projects with those programs.

Jim: That's interesting. What about data analysis using software programs?

Manju: For data analytics, software packages like SAS, Minitab, Tableau, R, Python, Excel, etc. are commonly used, though Tableau is useful as a visualization program. Many analytical techniques are part of these programs. The trick is to select suitable techniques for the intended purpose. For regular business people, the details of the techniques are far less important than understanding their purpose and it's relation to the results you desire.

Jim: Okay. Thanks, Manju. In our company, we are using Excel, R, Python, and Tableau quite a lot.

Manju: Makes sense. Lot of companies are using them. In some situations, to conduct detailed analysis and interpret results, individualized analytics platform, may be useful. This type of platform is intended for individualized analytics, which is different from other approaches.

Jim: Individualized analytics. I have never heard of it. Must be very useful.

Manju: Yes, Jim. Using individualized analytics, we can understand every individual's problem as opposed to viewing those individuals as part of a group (or population) with similar behavior patterns.

Jim: What do you mean by individual? Does this apply only to people?

Manju: No, Jim. Here individual means any entity – it could be a person, a service facility, a location, or a machine.

Jim: Understood. Thanks, Manju.

Manju: There are individualized analytics platforms, which provide a scale based on a number of variables and contribution of each variable to the problem. Using the scale, we can measure how far every individual is from the desired state. Higher values on the scale indicate performance problems. Contribution measures of the variables help focus on highly contributing variables to the individual problems. Such outputs can also provide improvement plans for the individuals, so corrective measures can be taken to resolve these issues.

Jim: This is very interesting, Manju. I think understanding such outputs will be easy. Even people like me can easily understand and put them to use. In other words, one can easily perform data science activities and deploy results without help from data scientists.

Manju: That is exactly my point, Jim! Such outputs will allow regular business people to take actions very easily since interpretation process is simplified.

Outcome Analysis

Now we need to discuss what needs to be done after data analysis.

Jim: Once data analysis is done, shouldn't we go ahead and use the insights in the decision-making activities?

Manju: Not yet, Jim. After conducting the data analysis, the following questions need to be addressed:

1. How reliable is the information from the analysis?
2. How much of this information is relevant to the problem?

Jim: Oh, Okay. How do we address these questions?

Manju: I think, to address the first question, RQI could be very useful. To address the second question, practicality of the information to the problem is very important. The practicality aspects of the solutions need to be considered while implementing them. You may have a mathematically elegant answer, but it is of no use if it cannot be implemented in practice.

Jim: Manju, understood. I think this is where subject matter expertise and experience will come into play.

Manju: Yes, Jim. Subject matter expertise and experience will help in fine tuning an analytical solution to practically feasible one. Just data science knowledge alone will not be adequate for this purpose. Lack of practicality aspects would make a very good data science solution fail.

Individualized Analytics for Eat Healthy Problem

Now if we think about Eat Healthy's problem, the main goal is to improve sales percentages in the five non-performing locations. As mentioned earlier, suppose they use population, ethnicity, average household income, desire to eat healthy food, and discounts/coupons offered as probable root cause drivers. Here, using the individualized analytics approach may be their best bet. Note that here each location represents an individual entity.

Jim: Sounds interesting. I think the individualized analytics approach will be quite helpful for us.

Manju: Can you get data on drivers such as population, ethnicity, average household income, desire to eat healthy food, discounts/coupons etc., for both performing and non-performing locations? Using these data, I want demonstrate how individualized analytics will help solve Eat Healthy's problem.

Jim: Sure. I can get this data. I will make sure to bring good quality data as well. I will also make sure that the data that was sent earlier on ethnicity and discounts/coupons (when we were discussing data quality aspects) is fixed. Do you want to meet in one week's time to continue our discussion?

Manju: Sounds good to me. See you in one week.

(Jim gets the data sets that Manju asked for and meets with her in a week).

Jim: Good afternoon, Manju. How are you?

Manju: I am good, Jim. I am looking forward to our discussion. Did you get the data I asked for?

Jim: Yes. Here are the data files.

Manju: Awesome. These data files look good. The data seem to be complete and valid. Let's use the individualized analytics approach to see what variables are contributing most to the non-performing locations.

Jim: Sounds good.

Manju: We can run individualized analytics and build a measurement scale. The base or reference for this scale is from performing locations. Higher the value on the scale indicates a higher deviation from the desired state (in this example performing locations). Using this scale, the performance of various locations can be measured. Let me run individualized analytics for this data.

Jim: Looking forward to seeing the results.

(Manju takes few minutes to load data into a software program and runs individualized analytics).

Manju: Jim, as you can see this from Table 4.3, the non-performing locations have higher scale values, indicating that they are very far from the performing locations. I also conducted a root cause analysis to identify important drivers with contribution percentages of these drivers to the scale value. This is also provided in Table 4.3. I just want to reiterate that I used a software package to conduct these analyses. With the right kind of data, anyone can run these analyses if they have the suitable tools.

Jim: Okay. Got it. Can you explain root cause analysis in little more detail, Manju?

Manju: Sure. Root cause analysis is used to identify the drivers causing the problem. Basically through root cause analysis, you will understand where things are going wrong. In the context of Eat Healthy's example, the drivers are listed in Table 4.3 with

TABLE 4.3

Scale Values and Contribution Driver Percentages for Non-Performing Locations

Location	Scale Values	Population	Ethnicity	Household Income	Desire for Healthy Food	Discounts/ Coupons
Location 5	87.5	2.09	53.82	6.50	3.77	33.82
Location 11	88.2	2.65	48.25	5.50	15.35	28.25
Location 17	86.75	1.68	60.02	4.32	8.06	25.92
Location 18	89.3	4.09	45.32	7.10	13.17	30.32
Location 24	90.12	1.08	46.92	4.70	7.28	40.02

their percentage contributions to their scale values. In this table, contributions above 10% are highlighted (bold). The most succinct description of root cause analysis I've seen comes from an old African proverb:

Do not look where you fell, but instead you should examine where you slipped.

Jim: Great. I got it now. This is the essence of root cause driver analysis.

Manju: Okay. As you can see from Table 4.3, the scale values of non-performing locations are coming from two drivers – ethnicity and discounts/coupons. Also, desired to eat healthy is somewhat significant in two of the non-performing locations.

Jim: I see that, Manju. This is the type of analysis we are looking for. The approach is simple and easy to interpret. Very interesting.

Manju: I am glad you realized this. Since ethnicity and discounts/coupons are important drivers, we can look at the data for these variables and compare them using performing locations and non-performing locations. Let us compare this with one non-performing location. We can use the same location information that we used earlier when we were discussing data quality issues (Chapter 3). The comparison data is shown in Table 4.4. Jim, can you see anything different in Table 4.4.

Jim: Manju, looking at this data, I see more Asians coming to this location and also many customers did not get discounts/coupons.

Manju: Absolutely, Jim. You are correct. I quickly calculated some numbers. About 64% customers visiting this location are Asians and only 12% Asians visited performing locations. In addition, only 40% of customers in this location received discounts/coupons and about 80% of customers received coupons/discounts in performing locations. I also looked at data corresponding to other locations that you provided. I got similar results for other locations as well.

Jim: Sounds great, Manju. To get to the results in Table 4.3, I think we need some sophisticated tools though results are easy to interpret. However, the analysis you performed with Table 4.4 is a simple old school way of looking at performing and non-performing locations and understanding the differences.

TABLE 4.4

Sample Data Corresponding to Ethnicity and Discounts/Coupons for Both Types of Locations

Performing Locations			Non-Performing Locations		
Customer	Ethnicity	Discounts/Coupons	Customer	Ethnicity	Discounts/Coupons
1	White	Yes	1	White	No
2	White	Yes	2	Hispanic	Yes
3	African American	No	3	White	Yes
4	White	No	4	Asian	No
5	African American	Yes	5	Asian	No
6	African American	Yes	6	Asian	No
7	Hispanic	Yes	7	Asian	Yes
8	African American	Yes	8	Asian	No
9	Asian	Yes	9	Asian	Yes
10	White	Yes	10	Asian	No
11	White	No	11	Asian	Yes
12	Asian	Yes	12	African American	No
13	Hispanic	Yes	13	Asian	Yes
14	White	Yes	14	Hispanic	No
15	Black	Yes	15	White	No
16	White	Yes	16	White	No
17	White	Yes	17	Hispanic	Yes
18	African American	No	18	White	Yes
19	White	No	19	Asian	No
20	African American	Yes	20	Asian	No
21	African American	Yes	21	Asian	No
22	Hispanic	Yes	22	Asian	Yes
23	African American	Yes	23	Asian	No
24	Asian	Yes	24	Asian	Yes
25	White	Yes	25	Asian	No

Manju: You are correct, Jim. We need some good tools to process data and after narrowing down analytics results, and sometimes we need to resort to an old school way to compare and take suitable actions to solve these problems. This is very important and any one can easily follow old school logic, there is no rocket science involved here.

Jim: Wow. This is very interesting. You are making me more and more confident with your descriptions and analyses. Thank you.

Manju: No problem, Jim.

Jim: Are there any other tools for conducting root cause analysis?

Manju: There are tools. Sometimes root cause driver analysis can be performed using simple tools like a cause and effect diagram.

> A cause and effect diagram is a simple listing of all potential causes (drivers) and identifying root cause drivers through further data analysis. This was proposed by Dr. Ishikawa of Japan. Since this diagram resembles a fish bone, it is also called a fishbone diagram.

Jim: Interesting. Can we create a fishbone diagram for Eat Healthy's problem?

Manju: Absolutely. Here, a fishbone diagram helps us find our way through various activities that will be affecting sales in a given location. The fishbone diagram shown below (in Figure 4.3) lists all possible causes that impact sales. For all the main causes such as people and location, sub-causes are listed corresponding to them.

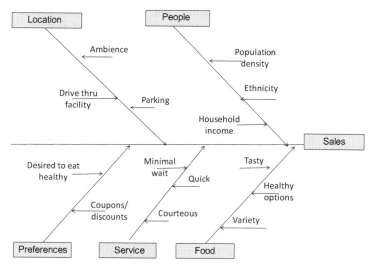

FIGURE 4.3
Fishbone diagram for sales.

Jim: Yes. It does look like a fishbone. It shows all causes in a comprehensive manner.

Manju: True, Jim. From the list of all potential causes, root cause drivers can be determined by further analysis with data.

Jim: Now I am planning to take the results you provided in Tables 4.3 and 4.4, and talk to our team and senior leaders.

Manju: That is what I was going to suggest as well. Please validate the results with your team and talk to your management to get their feedback. This will be your task for our next meeting. We can meet again in three days if it works for you.

Jim: It definitely works, Manju. Since this is an important problem, I can easily get time on peoples' calendars. Thanks so much Manju for this analysis.

(Jim takes results to discuss them with his team and senior leaders. He meets Manju after three days).

Manju: Good to see you again, Jim. Any progress on the Eat Healthy's project discussions?

Jim: Yes, we had great discussions based on the results you provided. After further analysis, we identified that in these five locations there are large Asian communities. We then came to the conclusion that if we took measures to attract those potential customers in the area, we may increase sales. As a result, we decided to add traditional Asian spices to the plant-based items and also give our customers more discounts/coupons.

Manju: Great. See with good data analysis, we can take effective decisions quickly. I am glad you all are on the same page now. Only data-based decisions will help us reach a consensus so quickly. With regard to discounts/coupons, Eat Healthy may use artificial intelligence (AI) methods to determine how much discounts will attract various customers with similar backgrounds.

Jim: That will be a wonderful thing to do. We can automate the system and predict customer preferences, although it may be a long way to go for us.

Manju: That may be true. But eventually it can be done. After taking your findings and potential solutions to senior leaders to get their approval, changes can be made as necessary.

Jim: Do you think this approach will certainly increase sales by 7.5% for the underperforming locations?

Manju: We don't know yet. We have now entered the testing phase of the process. Although the goal is in six months, you will know earlier whether they are on track to hitting that goal. If they are, then the analysis worked. If you find that you aren't getting much closer to the target sales numbers (7.5% in this case), there may be a problem with the drivers you chose, and you must select other drivers and re-initiate the process.

Jim: Okay. What's next, Manju?

Manju: Jim, I forgot to tell you. Throughout next six months, I will be tied up with my trips to India and Japan for my personal projects. I will be leaving next week. I will be back after three months for a couple of weeks. At that time, we can review the effect of the actions taken and discuss other topics related to data science.

Jim: Sounds good. I remember you taking trips to these countries last year around this time. Do you want me to do anything in particular in the next three months?

Manju: Of course, I have some work for you, Jim. Now that we have completed our discussions about three phases and associated game plans to solve data science problems, I want you to keep reviewing the game plans/strategies that we have discussed. In addition, you and your team should monitor the effectiveness of the actions your guys are planning to take to increase sales in non-performing locations throughout the next six months.

Jim: Okay, Manju. I will review the game plan/strategies and my team, and I will monitor the impact of our actions on sales. I will meet you after three months. Have a safe trip.

Manju: Thanks, Jim. If you need anything from me, please call or text me.

(Manju and Jim will reconvene after three months)

Jim: Hi, Manju. So good to see you. How are things?

Manju: Things are fine. It's good to be back with you again.

Jim: As I was updating our progress periodically while you were away, within the last three months, the five non-performing locations started to perform better due to our actions. Everyone is so pleased, although we have not yet reached 7.5% sales increase

TABLE 4.5

% Sales Increase in the Five Under Performing
Locations (in 3 months)

Location	% Sales Increase after 3 Months
Location 5	5.12
Location 11	5.57
Location 17	5.02
Location 18	5.48
Location 24	4.97

mark. We all think we are in the right direction to achieve our target. Table 4.5 shows the results for the five locations. The average increased to 5.23%.

Manju: That's so nice, Jim. Looks like your plan is working well. Keep monitoring the results and I am sure you will hit your target in six months.

Jim: Sounds good, Manju. What data science topics are we going to discuss today?

Manju: I will tell you about it. First, let me ask you this question. When you are working on some important activity, whether it be working on sending your child to a college or accumulating funds for mortgage down payment, how do you accomplish it? What steps would you take?

Jim: Let me answer this based on my experience. First, I will create a plan and come up with a process. After that I will follow the process steps in a disciplined manner to achieve the overall goal.

Manju: Excellent, Jim. That is the answer I was expecting. Your answer will actually be my next topic. Today I will start with a discussion regarding the project structure and its importance to data science projects.

Jim: That sounds wonderful.

5

Project Structure

DATA SCIENCE PROJECT STRUCTURE

Manju: Let me start the discussion about the importance of project structure for data science projects. The goal of data science should be to help individuals/organizations to process data so they can make better decisions through analytical outcomes. This requires clear problem description, goal statement, some software packages/technologies, and resources with a sound structure. Structure is very much required to perform analytics quickly and efficiently.

> If you can't describe what you are doing as a process you don't know what you're doing.
> **–W.E. Deming (Source: AZ quotes)**

You may have several good ideas but in order to select the best one and execute, you need to have a structure in place. Structure helps us define our activities, prioritize them, and execute them in a disciplined way. The goal statement is important to help you get to where you want to be but the structure actually takes you there. In that sense, structure may be the most important part of a data science project. Many initiatives fail due to a lack of structure and a disciplined execution. Hence in data science activities, structure plays a very important role. Structure is a necessity in order to execute data science projects with high-quality analytics. The phases we have discussed so far provide us that structure for solving data science projects.

DOI: 10.4324/9781003165279-5

Jim: Yes, Manju. Structure is critical for anything we do. I am big fan of the New England Patriots. I always think they perform well because of the good structure that exists within the organization. I think the hallmarks of their structure include discipline, enforcing the idea of doing your job and doing things right the first time. I believe, though other teams have better players, the Patriots are more successful because of these qualities. I also want to add that structure is important in making our families successful as well. Without structure, things can go out of control, which will cause several issues while impacting the families in a negative manner.

Manju: I am 100% in agreement with you on this Jim. The structure I described for running data science projects is similar to the Six Sigma based project structure that is used in process improvement activities. The Six Sigma projects are executed through the DMAIC (Define, Measure, Analyze, Improve and Control) phases.

Jim: Manju, can you explain Six Sigma more in detail? This is an important concept.

Manju: Sure! Six Sigma is a process-oriented approach that is aimed at minimizing waste and maximizing process efficiency. Six Sigma uses a set of managerial, engineering, and analytical concepts.

SIX SIGMA PROCESS-ORIENTED APPROACH

Motorola was an early adopter of Six Sigma improvement activities to gain a competitive advantage and later on companies such as General Electric and Bank of America began using Six Sigma methodologies extensively. Typically, Six Sigma projects are executed through the DMAIC (Define, Measure, Analyze, Improve and Control) phases.

In DMAIC-based Six Sigma approach, first the problem is defined; in the Measure phase, the extent of the problem is measured; in the Analyze phase, the problem is analyzed by identifying causes of the problem; in the improve phase, solutions to the problem are identified; and finally in control phase, the improvements are monitored and controlled. If you think

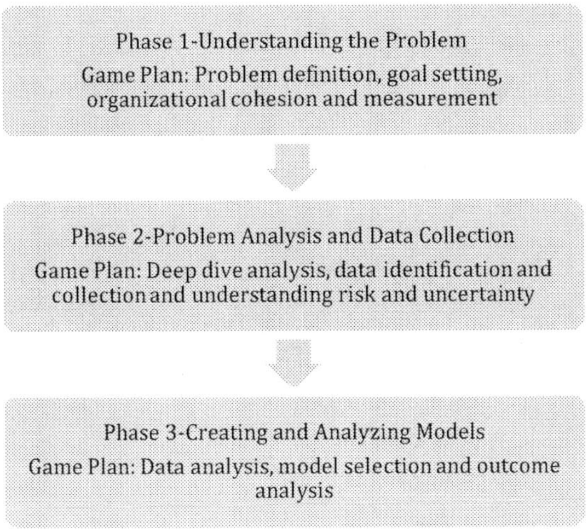

FIGURE 5.1
Data science project structure

about the three-phase approach I described for data science projects, it is similar to DMAIC approach.

Jim: That sounds right to me Manju. Your approach is similar to DMAIC approach.

Manju: So far, we have discussed the important phases of a data science project along with the structure required for its execution. Figure 5.1 is a consolidation of the three phases.

Jim: This is great Manju. I also want to see how these game plans/strategies are applied to other problems.

Manju: Jim, you read my mind. I am planning to do that any way. Let me describe a couple of success stories based on real-world problems. I'll use Figure 5.1 to highlight these problems and their solutions.

Jim: Great! I think it would be very helpful to see other examples using this type of structure.

6

Data Science Stories

Manju: I chose these two case examples because they both used the three-phase approach that we discussed. Although both case studies are addressing different problems than Eat Healthy, the process of solving the problem was similar.

Jim: Sounds good.

Manju: Let me start with health management case example.

Case Example 1: Proactive Detection and Diagnosis of Overall Health

PHASE 1: UNDERSTANDING THE PROBLEM

PROBLEM DEFINITION

Health management for individuals is extremely important as undiagnosed issues frequently result in high cost due to expensive advanced care treatments, and sometimes they could also result in the loss of lives. It is important to diagnose health issues in their early stages and understand the significant variables impacting one's overall health. So, a medical facility chose to improve the process of diagnosing various health issues so that problems can be proactively determined and resolved at an early stage through a better health management system. So they came up with the following goal statement.

Goal Statement: *To design a mechanism that measures the overall health in individual patients and determine significant variables affecting the health in a three-month time frame.*

DOI: 10.4324/9781003165279-6

Jim: Here the specific quantification of goals is not possible since the main purpose is to build a measurement system, which did not exist before, right?

Manju: Absolutely, Jim. That is what I was going to say. What do you think about other aspects of goal statement?

Jim: I think other aspects are taken care of. Design of a mechanism to measure overall health addresses the aspect of measurement and timeframe is also mentioned.

Manju: Good, Jim. That's quite right.

ORGANIZATIONAL COHESION AND MEASUREMENT

A medical specialist led this effort with a small team, which can be considered as the data science team. When it comes to health measurement, the main purpose is to measure the overall health of the patients and determine actions. Since the target metric here should accurately measure the overall health by developing a measurement system, capability and potential of the metric are not applicable. Do you agree?

Jim: Sounds good to me.

Manju: Now let me start phase 2 of this case example.

PHASE 2: ANALYZING THE PROBLEM AND COLLECTING DATA

DEEP DIVE ANALYSIS AND DATA IDENTIFICATION AND COLLECTION

As we know in phase 2, the first step in this phase is to perform a deep dive analysis. For this purpose, it is important to understand the variables that influence the overall health and build a measurement system using them. Several variables including age, height, weight, total cholesterol, LDL cholesterol, HDL cholesterol, triglycerides, blood pressure, and the number of hours of sleep were considered. The data corresponding to these variables was collected and ensured for good quality. Using this data corresponding to various individuals, a measurement system was developed. Here, measurements were taken from group of individuals that did not have health issues (desired state).

Jim: Manju, development of measurement system and taking measurements from the individuals that did not have health issues reminds me of the approach we have taken for Eat Healthy. In Eat Healthy case the measurements were taken from performing locations.

Manju: Good observation Jim. You are correct. The approach is the same. In Eat Health case individuals correspond to locations and here individuals correspond to patients.

Now let us focus on risk and uncertainty aspects of this study.

UNDERSTANDING THE RISK AND UNCERTAINTY

As in the Eat Healthy example, three most important risks were identified. Jim, do you recall the three types?

Jim: Certainly, Manju. The three important risks are:

1. Risk and uncertainty in data measurement errors
2. Risk and uncertainty due to the existence of variation
3. Risk and uncertainty in prediction, diagnosis, and decision-making

Manju: Excellent, Jim. Those are the three risks.

To handle the first risk – the team ensured measurements on the variables are accurate and reliable by making sure that the underlying measurement systems are accurate and precise. This helped the team ensure that the data is fit for the intended purpose and ready for analytics.

For the risk due to existence of variation, they ensured that the observations in the desired state are as uniform as possible since they are coming from people without any health issues.

Jim: Is this because the scale values are measured from the desired state, which corresponds to healthy individuals?

Manju: You nailed it Jim.

For the risk and uncertainty in prediction, diagnosis, and decision-making, the team ensured that all the possible errors corresponding to relevant variables are taken into consideration as they were assumed to be influencing the measurement scale and hence the overall health. In addition, team also studied uncontrollable or noise factors and their impact.

Jim: Sounds good. Good description Manju.

Manju: Thanks Jim. Now let's start phase 3.

PHASE 3: CREATING AND ANALYZING MODELS
DATA ANALYSIS AND MODEL SELECTION

Since the intention here is to build a measurement system for measuring overall health and identifying significant variables impacting the health for individual patients, the individualized measurement scale approach was used.

Jim: Got it. Similar to the Eat Healthy example-right?
Manju: Yes. That is true.

The data science team built a measurement scale based on the data on selected variables. The reference for this scale is based on all of these variables for healthy patients (desired state). As I mentioned before, higher scale values indicate a higher degree of abnormality or unhealthiness. Table 6.1, shows the drivers corresponding to a sample set of patients with health issues. Note that these individuals also have higher values of scale indicating that they are abnormals or have health issues. Table 6.1 also provides details of variation analysis and contribution percentages of variables impacting the scale. In this table, values above 5% contributions are highlighted (bold).

Jim: Is there any reason why they chose 5% as cut-off?
Manju: I will get to that soon.
Jim: Okay. Manju, let me understand Table 6.1. The row corresponding to scale provides overall health measurement values for the individuals and rows corresponding to variables display their percent contributions for the scale values, right?
Manju: You got it, Jim. This is similar to the Eat Healthy example that we discussed earlier (Table 4.3 in particular). Here, since it is a health-related study, to be more cautious, variables with 5% or more contributions were highlighted (bold) in Table 6.1. It's worth noting that scale values for individuals will also help us prioritize the patients with a higher degree of abnormalities and treat them accordingly.
Jim: Got it, Manju. I understand now why they chose 5% as cut-off. It is really interesting and Table 6.1 is very easy to interpret, and one can easily take actions on the variables that are impacting health.

TABLE 6.1

Important Variables and Their Percent Contributions to the Sample of Five Individuals/Patients (Along with Scale Values)

Notation	Variable	Individual 1	Individual 2	Individual 3	Individual 4	Individual 5
Scale values		60.5	44.2	45.1	38.0	49.2
X1	Total cholesterol (%)	1.87	0.60	4.95	**13.07**	1.13
X2	LDL cholesterol (%)	3.75	2.85	1.72	0.24	0.02
X3	HDL cholesterol (%)	0.36	1.30	0.42	4.53	9.77
X4	Triglycerides (%)	**7.63**	0.95	**5.67**	4.25	2.20
X5	Non-HDL-C (%)	**10.47**	6.69	**21.36**	**9.08**	4.25
X6	ApoB (%)	2.72	**6.26**	2.61	0.14	**8.26**
X7	sdLDL-C (%)	0.65	1.21	3.65	1.21	1.94
X8	%sdLDL-C (%)	2.87	0.01	**8.95**	3.84	4.45
X9	VLDL-C (%)	0.70	**7.49**	1.01	3.95	0.44
X10	Lp(a) (%)	1.44	**6.68**	0.24	0.01	2.85
X11	ApoA-1 (%)	0.14	**29.30**	0.00	0.78	0.46
X12	High sensitivity CRP (%)	0.33	0.04	0.63	**13.90**	**7.32**
X13	ESR (%)	0.00	**7.05**	0.63	0.78	0.00
X14	HbA1c (%)	0.04	**6.85**	2.55	0.01	**5.22**
X15	Glucose (%)	**11.43**	0.23	0.90	0.04	**7.08**
X16	Insulin (%)	**12.11**	0.31	0.53	**10.29**	2.60
X17	Mercury (%)	0.14	0.07	0.00	0.08	0.09
X18	Height (%)	2.21	3.30	2.46	1.77	0.21

(*Continued*)

TABLE 6.1 (Continued)

Important Variables and Their Percent Contributions to the Sample of Five Individuals/Patients (Along with Scale Values)

Notation	Variable	Individual 1	Individual 2	Individual 3	Individual 4	Individual 5
X19	Weight (%)	6.75	0.58	1.80	0.29	5.27
X20	BMI (%)	5.31	0.69	14.25	2.25	9.16
X21	Waist circumference (%)	11.73	0.79	1.05	9.51	1.78
X22	Most recent blood pressure reading-upper (%)	0.61	7.34	5.89	11.66	0.03
X23	Most recent blood pressure reading-lower (%)	11.85	2.52	1.22	0.61	18.46
X24	Minutes of exercise/week (%)	1.02	1.67	0.19	1.28	0.37
X25	Hours of sleep/night (%)	2.10	2.69	15.33	5.04	5.13
X26	Cadmium (%)	1.77	2.53	1.97	1.41	1.51

Manju: Absolutely. I am glad you pointed it out. Now let's discuss outcome analysis.

OUTCOME ANALYSIS

This scale has been in use. Improvement plans are put in place for the
individuals to treat risks associated with their overall health. For every
individual, important variables are monitored and controlled in order
to ensure the numbers are improving and these patients are progressing
toward a healthy state.

Jim: Got it. I have another question. How did they validate the measurement system? Was any measure used?
Manju: Good question. The measurements were validated with patients
with known health issues while building the analytics approach.
This is how they validated quality of analytics.

Now let's move on next case example that I planned to discuss.

Jim: Great. I am looking forward to it

Case Example 2: Improving Customer Satisfaction by Building a Predictive Model

Manju: Jim, note that this example is a bit broader, it may be the most
applicable to you as it addresses a more common issue.
Jim: Got it Manju. Seems like an interesting problem.
Manju: I think so too! Let me start with phase 1 of the data science
approach for this example.

PHASE 1: UNDERSTANDING THE PROBLEM

PROBLEM DEFINITION

It is quite important to understand customer expectations and measure
their satisfaction levels. In our data-driven and data-collecting world, we
have access to quite a lot of customer data. In this case, the marketing unit of
a company wants to improve their existing customer satisfaction levels and
subsequently predict customer satisfaction by building a analytical model.

First, customer satisfaction was measured based on customer surveys
using a scale from 1 to 10 with 10 indicating the highest level of satisfaction.

After doing this, they found that the existing satisfaction level was at 7. From here, the team built models using relevant variables. These variables include the indicators of level of service, issue resolution time, mobile services, and demographic information.

Jim, any thoughts on problem definition.

Jim: I think it's clear. They want to improve existing level of customer satisfaction and build a model to identify impacting variables to improve satisfaction level. In addition, they want to use the model for predictive purposes so proactive actions can be taken as needed. Am I correct?

Manju: True. You got it. Since this study was intended to develop a quantitative model to improve customer satisfaction, a goal statement for this project was as follows:

Goal Statement: *To build and deploy a sustainable model in four months to improve customer satisfaction by 2 points and subsequently use this model to predict customer satisfaction.*

Jim: The goal statement is very clear. They covered all relevant aspects of a good goal statement.

Manju: I agree.

ORGANIZATIONAL COHESION AND MEASUREMENT

A project team was formed involving all relevant people and a charter was created with resources, scope, clear roles, and responsibilities. As mentioned before, the current level of satisfaction was at 7, which represents the "actual" performance in metrics terminology. The team's "target" was 9, which is the performance goal.

Jim: Did they also evaluate the capability corresponding to customer satisfaction?

Manju: Yes. That is what I am about to speak. The team constructed a control chart for the average customer satisfaction metric based on the last twelve months of data. This was done to calculate the "capability" of this process by looking at some special causes. The control chart is as shown in Figure 6.1.

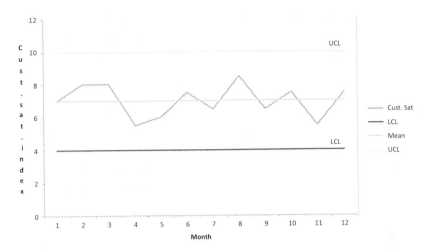

FIGURE 6.1
Control chart for customer satisfaction index.

Jim, any observations on the control chart?

Jim: By looking at the control chart using Figure 6.1, it is clear that the process is in control and that there are no special causes. Does this indicate for this situation, "actual" performance and "capability" are the same?

Manju: Yes. That was the situation. Here "actual" and "capability" correspond to the same value. So, the team started to look at the overall process to identify impacting variables causing the variation in customer satisfaction.

Jim: So, this step is actually part of phase 2, problem analysis, and data collection-right?

Manju: Yes. That is what we will discuss now.

PHASE 2: ANALYZING THE PROBLEM AND COLLECTING DATA

DEEP DIVE ANALYSIS AND DATA IDENTIFICATION AND COLLECTION

The team studied a number of variables that could be impacting customer satisfaction. These variables include the indicators of level of service, issue resolution time, mobile services, price competitiveness, their demographic information, etc. The data corresponding to these variables was collected. The team also performed data quality analysis to ensure that the data is fit for use.

Any questions, Jim?

Jim: No, Manju. Clear to me.

Manju: Alright. Now let's briefly discuss risk and uncertainty aspects related to this case example.

UNDERSTANDING THE RISK AND UNCERTAINTY

The three types of risks discussed in the first case example are applicable here as well. They are:

1. Risk and uncertainty in data measurement errors the team ensured measurements on the variables are accurate and reliable through a robust measurement system.
2. Risk and uncertainty due to existence of variation – this was addressed through control chart analysis for the customer satisfaction metric (Figure 6.1) and the variables under study.
3. Risk and uncertainty in prediction, diagnosis, and decision-making for this, the team ensured that all possible errors corresponding to relevant variables were taken care and the team also studied uncontrollable or noise factors and their impact to the customer satisfaction.

Manju: Jim, is there any other type of risk and uncertainty that we should be looking at here or the above three types that I mentioned just now are adequate?

Jim: Let me think. I have a feeling that the team has one additional type of risk here. Is it risk and uncertainty due to procrastination?

Manju: Exactly! Do you know why?

Jim: If they build a great model and do not deploy it, it becomes waste of time, effort, and resources.

Manju: That's quite correct Jim. That was the fourth type of risk the team had considered.

Now let us move on phase 3 of the data science approach.

PHASE 3: CREATING AND ANALYZING MODELS

DATA ANALYSIS AND MODEL SELECTION

The purpose of this study was to improve the customer satisfaction index by two points and predict the same through a model by understanding root cause drivers (variables). After having a series of discussions on the model selection, the team decided to use regression analysis. Do you know what regression analysis is?

Jim: Only heard of it. Could you briefly explain it?

Manju: Sure, in the context of this example, regression analysis helps us create an equation between the customer satisfaction index and the root cause drivers (variables). The equation will be of the form $Y = b + a1X1 + a2X2 + a3X3 + ...$, where Y is customer satisfaction index (called dependent variables), X1, X2, X3... are the drivers (called independent variables) impacting the index, and a1, a2,.., a3 are called coefficients of X.

Jim: Manju, this is becoming somewhat mathematical now. Can you talk in simple terms and explain a bit more about the regression equation $Y = b + a1X1 + a2X2 + a3X3 + ...$, with an example?

Manju: Sure, Jim. Let us say that we have an equation for customer satisfaction index with the following form:

Customer satisfaction index, $(Y) = 0.8 + 0.25 *$ service level $+ 3 *$ issue resolution time $+ 5 *$ price competitiveness $+ .....$ Using this equation, one can calculate or predict customer satisfaction index by using values associated with variables related to service level, issue resolution time, price competitiveness, etc. In regression analysis, the significance of the variables on Y is determined by coefficients. If a coefficient is significant, then the corresponding variable is significant and hence impacts the Y.

Jim: Okay. Through the coefficients and analysis, we can determine the impact of these variables on the customer satisfaction index, right?

Manju: Exactly.

Jim: How do we determine if a coefficient is significant?

Manju: Good question. Usually for every coefficient a quantity called p-value is computed. If the p-value is low as compared to a level of significance (usually 5% or 0.05) then it indicates that the corresponding variable is significant. All statistical programs provide p-value information in the regression analysis output.

Jim: Got it, Manju. Thank you.

Manju: Sure. So, this way the team built a decent regression model by understanding impact of important variables and that can also be used for future predictions.

Jim: Do I need to know how to develop the regression equation in detail?

Manju: Not at all. I just wanted to give you a brief overview on it. All you need to know is these type of problems can be solved by regression analysis. All software packages will be able to perform regression analysis. I just wanted you to know what logic is behind regression analysis, what the software packages will do and how you can interpret the results.

Jim: Sounds great, Manju. How much improvement was made in this case? Did they hit the target?

Manju: That is what I am going to talk about in the outcome analysis Jim.

OUTCOME ANALYSIS

Through this model, the customer satisfaction index was improved by 1 point (the average index went up to 8 points from 7). From here, there need to be an additional work to get the additional point so they hit their goal.

Jim: Manju, does this mean this model is not the best. What is the best?

Manju: No model is the best. This model is useful to improve the satisfaction index to 8. There is a famous remark by statistician, George E. P. Box , *"Essentially, all models are wrong, but some are useful (Welsing, 2015)."* That's not meant to sound discouraging, but to illustrate that there won't be a perfect model to solve any issue. The regression model they built is definitely useful but, for further improvement, a different model or other variables need to be considered. This is how we can continuously improve models.

Jim: Got it.

Manju: This completes the discussion of about second case example.

Jim: This is very interesting. I learnt quite a lot during these sessions. I think it will be a good idea to review all the concepts you explained.

Manju: I like your idea Jim. That's very important.

Jim: Great! Let's do that then.

7

Concept Review

Manju: Before we begin reviewing the concepts highlighted, I would like to know if you have any questions.

Jim: Manju, I want you to address one question: How much data should one use for obtaining good insights?

Manju: Great question! This question is particularly very important as we are now in the big data era and have access to lot of data. In my view, most data science projects don't require a lot of data. A small set of data is adequate for drawing meaningful insights that can easily be implemented. Deriving insights with minimal data helps ensure that the subsequent decisions that are reached can be enacted feasibly.

Jim: Makes sense. Thanks so much.

Manju: No problem. Now my question to you is: what do you think about the data science? My hope is, after these discussions, you feel confident to address the issues within your organization using these concepts and approaches. The topic of data science can be intimidating, but the concepts when broken down are quite simple to understand and can be used by anyone within an organization. By nature, we use and produce data every day. The game plans we discussed coupled with practical experience should help people become productive data problem-solvers. The fear of data science is often times the largest hurdle to overcome, and my hope is to dispel myths about its complexity and lay out the basics so that all members of an organization can use data science to solve data problems effectively.

DOI: 10.4324/9781003165279-7

Jim: Very true, Manju. These discussions have cleared up a lot of confusion and misconceptions I've had. I feel pretty confident in taking what I've learned here and using it to help Eat Healthy and myself too in future projects.

Manju: Good to know that. Now, as we planned let's review the concepts that we discussed.

Jim: Sounds great.

CONCEPT REVIEW

Manju: Let us start reviewing the concepts phase-wise.

Phase 1: Understanding the Problem

It is an extraordinary thing, of course, that everybody is answering questions without knowing what the questions are. In other words, everybody is finding some remedy without knowing what the malady is

–Jawaharlal Nehru (Source: Rao, 1989)

1. Problem definition is extremely important to ensure that we are addressing the right problem and keep us focused on the problem at hand. For any data science project, the most important thing is to define the problem that we want to solve. This is where most projects fail since people will be working not knowing what they are working toward. Most "problem solving" solutions result in companies creating initiatives or actions in the name of improvement without properly defining what it is they are trying to improve.

   > Well defined goal along with a good project charter will bring all people together and ensures all are working towards the same goal

2. Like problem definition, goals must be clearly defined and communicated. Goals and subsequently your goal statement should be Specific (to the point), Measurable, Doable (Attainable), Realistic and should possess a Time aspect

(time to achieve the goal). Proper use of these aspects will result in the creation of a clear goal statement. A project charter is important as it will ensure organizational cohesion by formally establishing the scope, objectives, resources, expected business

> When you can measure what you are speaking about, and express it in numbers, you know something about it; but, when you cannot express it in numbers, your knowledge is of a meager and unsatisfactory kind
> **–Lord Kelvin (Source: Hubbard, 2010)**

value, role clarity, timeframes, and core deliverables.

3. After the problem definition and goal setting, it is important to focus on measurement. We need to measure the right things (metrics) to effectively solve problems. In the context of measurement, we need to consider following three aspects of a metric (Figure 7.1):

   i. **Target:** This indicates target performance level, which is the ultimate destination;

   ii. **Capability:** Attainable performance level, after removing the special causes of variation;

   iii. **Actual:** Actual performance level in the presence of special cause variation.

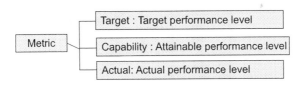

FIGURE 7.1
Three aspects of a metric.

These aspects help us understand where we stand currently, what our capability is and how far are we from our target. With a correct problem definition and the right kind of measurement, I think anyone can solve data problems.

Jim, did we miss any important topic in phase 1?

Jim: I don't think so, Manju. I think you covered it well.
Manju: Thanks, Jim. Let's review concepts in phase 2.

Phase 2: Analyzing the Problem and Collecting Data

Poor data quality will have very adverse effects in many forms in all activities we do with data.

1. Cross-examination of data/data quality is a quite important strategy. If you don't use good quality data, even spectacular analytical tools or approaches will not produce desired results. Quality over quantity is crucial for data. Further, poor data quality may incur losses in several forms. Most prominently, losing customer trust. Typically, data quality is measured in percentages based on four dimensions – completeness, conformity, validity, and accuracy. These percentages are called Data Quality scores (DQ scores). DQ scores are the indicators of the data performance. C.R Rao's checklist is very useful in ensuring data quality.

   Data is considered as an asset, and like any other asset a company acquires, you have to ensure it is of the quality you desire.

2. We must understand the issues causing the problem and find out possible root cause drivers through deep dive analysis. Deep dive analysis is basically understanding or examining possible root cause drivers of the problem.

   Anything else in phase 2, Jim?

Jim: I think you forgot about risk and uncertainty?

Manju: That's very important. Thanks for reminding about it.

3. There are ways to understand risk and uncertainty and mitigate them within a project but there is no way to fully eliminate them. Risk and uncertainty are part of life and business. Risk and uncertainties can come in

   > If we don't take into account risk and uncertainty in building models, they are bound to fail at some point even the models are developed in a sophisticated way by top-notch scientists.

   many forms. There are six sources of risk and uncertainty: (1) risk and uncertainty in data measurement errors; (2) risk and uncertainty due to existence of variation; (3) risk and uncertainty in prediction, diagnosis, and decision-making; (4) risk and uncertainty in analytics process execution; (5) risk and uncertainty due to incomplete information; and (6) risk and uncertainty due to procrastination.

Depending on the size of your business, some of these sources of risk may be more/less applicable than others. It is important to be aware of any and all sources of risk

> Any deviation from the target will result in poor quality and that is also a measure of loss to society
> **–Genichi Taguchi**

in order to avoid issues within your project. If we foresee and act, we can minimize the loss attributable to risk. We have to deal with risk and uncertainties everywhere, and life and data science are not exceptions. With the quantification of uncertainty and suitable mitigation actions, we can find better solutions that can be practically implemented.

4. Risk and uncertainty cause variation in product performance and analytical results, which will adversely impact the decision-making activities. Through the loss function concept, Genichi Taguchi established a relationship between variation and loss to the society. According to loss function, if product performance and analytical results deviate from the target, there is a loss. This loss can be in the form of product failures, customer dissatisfaction, company bankruptcies, loss of reputation, etc.

Jim: Agreed. Loss function concept is very interesting and important.
Manju: You are correct, Jim. Now let's review concepts in phase 3.

Phase 3: Creating and Analyzing Models

1. Data analytics should have purpose. That purpose should relate to question we are addressing and additional direction we would want to get from analytics.

Analytics = Providing insights for specific problems + Acquiring information for future activities (Rao, 1989)

> Statistics are often used as a drunkard uses lamppost-not to light his way but to support his instability
> **(Source: Batra, 1992)**

An important thing to note is that data analytics should be used for accomplishing something rather than to support what we already know.

Three important characteristics of analytics:
I. Simple to use and explain
II. Quickly scalable
III. Accurate and precise

The seven types of analytics (including the types that Gartner (2012) proposed):
I. Preparatory analytics
II. Descriptive analytics
III. Diagnostic analytics
IV. Cause-related analytics
V. Predictive analytics
VI. Prescriptive analytics
VII. Reliability-based analytics

2. All types of analytics that are discussed here are part of inferential analysis. In using inferential analysis, we will basically try to infer or predict the performance or extent of variability within a product or system by analyzing sample data. In other words, we use sample data to infer about large populations. Since we use sample data for inferences, the knowledge we gain from inferential analysis is uncertain and so we need to attach a degree of uncertainty or risk when we make conclusions. Dr. C.R. Rao (Rao, 1999) summarizes this as:

Usable Knowledge = Uncertain Knowledge + Knowledge of Uncertainty or Risk

3. In the overall analytics execution structure, three things are very important: (1) ensuring data quality; (2) validating analytical output with actual outcomes; and (3) senior management support.

Jim, would like to add anything here?

Jim: What about analytics quality?

Manju: That's what I was looking for. Thank you.

Quality of analytics is as important as quality of data.

4. Measuring the effectiveness of your analytics execution is very important. To measure the quality of analytics execution, the robust quality index (RQI) can be very useful. RQI is a holistic quality measure that includes data quality and analytics accuracy. RQI is measured on scale of 0–100, the higher number indicates better quality.

   After conducting the data analysis, two questions need to be addressed:

   i. How reliable is the information from the analysis?
   ii. How much of this information is relevant to the problem?

   The insights from data analytics should be deployed in decision-making activities, and they should be also be used in future activities. Data analytics should be continuously improved and updated with new information. Continuous improvement of data analytics will help make the models more and more useful.

Jim: So true, Manju.
Manju: Now let's move on to the last topic, project structure.

PROJECT STRUCTURE

Any effort without structure in place will not be as successful as we want it to be. Efforts with discipline and structure are bound to succeed.

1. The goal of data science should be to aid organizations process data so as to get better outcomes and make better business decisions.

   Processing data requires a structured approach along with sound technologies and good resources. These will help perform analytics quickly and efficiently. The

   > Achieving the goal is important but the structure you use to achieve the goal is more important.

   three-phase approach outlined in our discussion is well suited for executing a data science project.

2. The goal statement is important to get you to where you want to be, but the structure actually takes you there. In that sense, structure may be the most important part of a data science project.

Jim: Thanks, Manju. This review has been very helpful.

Manju: My pleasure, Jim! I am glad that review has been helpful for you. Since I will be traveling again soon, we can meet again in three months. Until then keep monitoring the performance of those five locations where you are working on improving sales.

Jim: Of course, I will do that, Manju.

(Jim and his team continue to monitor the performance in those five locations and Jim will meet Manju in three months with the results).

8

Manju and Jim's Concluding Meeting

Jim: Hey, Manju. How are you?

Manju: Hi, Jim. Finally I am back after finishing my personal projects. Good to see you.

Jim: Same here. We all did quite well with respect to our data science project. We reached our target sales increase numbers in all five locations through our actions. My team, senior leaders, and I are quite happy with the results. We all want to thank you for your help.

Manju: I am very glad to hear that. Can you share the results with me?

Jim: I know you would ask about the numbers. I have compiled the results of the last three quarters and they are in Table 8.1. I also drew a bar graph for sales in the three different time periods, shown in Figure 8.1. The average increase is 7.64%.

TABLE 8.1

% Sales Increase in Five Underperforming Locations (Latest Results)

Location	% Increase in Sales after 6 Months
Location 5	7.52
Location 11	8.2
Location 17	7.4
Location 18	7.65
Location 24	7.44

DOI: 10.4324/9781003165279-8

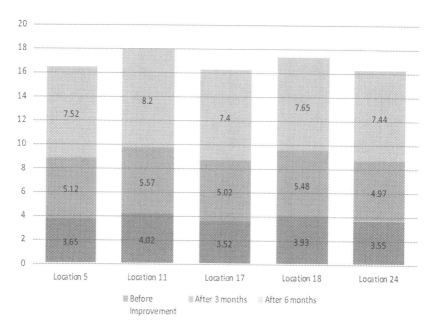

FIGURE 8.1
% sales increase in five underperforming locations.

Manju: Awesome, Jim. Let's look at them. On an average you exceeded the target (7.5%) and in one case you even reached 8.2%. Can you talk about how you implemented your actions?

Jim: Sure Manju. We knew that ethnicity and discounts/coupons were important drivers. Since a large number of Asians visit these locations, we started to add traditional Asian spices to the plant-based items while giving our customers more discounts/coupons. We used artificial intelligence (AI)based methods to determine what percentage of discounts will attract various individual customers and customers with similar backgrounds. These actions really worked. We are now in the process of continuing implementation of coupons/discount programs and using spices and condiments corresponding to the majority ethnicity in all 25 locations. We are pretty sure that very soon we will increase sales by more than 7.5% in all locations.

Manju: That's so great to hear. I am glad you guys worked on this and even brought in AI-based methods. Very nice.

Jim: Due to these results, my team and I were rewarded with generous incentives. Everyone in the team is so happy.

Manju: Wow! Your hard work paid off.

Jim: Your hard work too, Manju, I really want to thank you for taking the time to go through this with me.

Manju: I'm happy to do it!

Jim: You were right. There really isn't a lot of math involved, it was much simpler than I imagined.

Manju: I told you.

Jim: The cool thing is one can run a data science project if there is structure and discipline, that's all they need.

Manju: I completely agree. That is all you need!

Jim: Exactly.

Manju: The topic can feel overwhelming because many companies are relying more and more on data science.

Jim: Before starting this, we had almost no support from senior level management. I understood where they were coming from; you can't just throw money at projects without having some degree of confidence.

Manju: And now?

Jim: Well when you can go to them with data-backed solutions, it makes decision-making pretty easy.

Manju: So how do you feel about the data science process?

Jim: I wish I hadn't let my misconceptions keep me from talking to you about it years ago!

Manju: You know I'm not even a certified data scientist.

Jim: What?

Manju: Don't get me wrong, I read pretty extensively about it. But after teaching myself, I realized it's so much easier than I thought.

Jim: I have a request for you. Our senior leadership team is very impressed with our analysis. They want to appoint you as the data science advisor for Eat Healthy. Will you accept our invitation?

Manju: Absolutely, Jim. It will be my pleasure to serve as the data science advisor for Eat Healthy.

Jim: Okay. Thanks, Manju. I will tell them about your willingness to help us and they will initiate this process.

Manju: Sounds good.

Jim: Thanks again, Manju. I really don't know what I would have done if we hadn't talked.

Manju: Anytime. I think a lot of people probably feel as lost as you did. It's unfortunate because if they spent just a little time educating themselves, they would realize how accessible data science really is. If interested, anyone can be a data scientist. It just takes a few simple game plans/strategies and tools.

References

AZ Quotes, https://www.azquotes.com/author/3858-W_Edwards_Deming

AZ Quotes. n.d. https://www.azquotes.com/quote/811850.

Batra, Pramod 1992. *Management Thoughts*, Think Inc publication, London, UK.

Davenport, Thomas H. and Harris, Jeanne G. 2007. *Competing on Analytics- The New Science of Winning*, HBS Press, Boston, MA.

Deluzio, Mark C. 2020. *Flatlined*, Routledge (Productivity Press), Oxfordshire, UK.

Deming, W. E. 1989. *Out of the Crisis*, MIT Press, Cambridge, MA.

Deming, W. E. 1993. *The New Economics: For Industry, Government and Education*, MIT Press, Cambridge, MA.

Gartner. 2012. *Big Data Strategy Components: IT Essentials*, Gartner Publication, Stamford, CT. Published on 15th October 2012.

Harry, Mikel. *Philosophy*, https://www.mikeljharry.com/philosophy.php.

Harry, Mikel. 1997. *The Vision of Six Sigma: Tools and Methods for Breakthrough*, Tri Star-Boze Publications, Peoria, AZ.

Hubbard, Douglas W. 2010. *How to Measure Anything* (2nd Edition), John Wiley Publications, Hoboken, NJ.

Jugulum, Rajesh. 2014. *Competing with High Quality Data: Concepts, Tools and Techniques for Building a Successful Approach to Data Quality*, Wiley Publication, Hoboken, NJ.

Jugulum, Rajesh. 2018. *Robust Quality: Powerful Integration of Data Science and Process Engineering*, CRC Publication, Boca Raton, FL.

Rao, C. R. 1989. *Statistics and Truth: Putting Chance to Work*, Council of Scientific and Industrial Research (India) Publication, New Delhi, India.

Rao, C. R. 1999. *Statistics: A Technology for the Millennium*, Colloquium, organized by Department of Mathematics and Statistics, Oakland University, Michigan.

Redman, T. C. 1998. *The Impact of poor data quality on the typical enterprise. Communications of ACM*, 41(2), 191–204.

Redman, T. C. 2013. How to Start Thinking Like a Data Scientist. *Harvard Business Review*, November 2013.

Redman, T. C. 2021. *Seventeen Things That Will Help You Drive Meaningful Data Quality Improvement*. Lecture Notes (lecture given for the Northeastern Univ. Information analysis class students in November 2021).

Shewhart, Walter A. 1931. *Economic Control of Quality of Manufactured Product*, MacMillan Publishers.

Shewhart, Walter A. and Edwards Deming, W. (Foreword) 1986. *Statistical Method from the Viewpoint of Quality Control*, Dover Publication, Mineola, NY.

Taguchi, Genichi. 1986. *Introduction to Quality Engineering*, Asian Productivity Organization, Tokyo.

Taguchi, Genichi and Jugulam Rajesh. 1998-2005. Series of discussions between Taguchi and the author.

VivekaVani. 2019. *Swami Vivekananda's Quotes on Knowledge*, https://vivekavani.com/swami-vivekananda-quotes-knowledge/.

Welsing, Paco M. J. 2015. Statistical modelling: essentially, all models are wrong, but some are useful, Rheumatology, 54(7), 1133–1134.

Index

Note: **Bold** page numbers refer to tables and *italic* page numbers refer to figures.

Printed in the United States
by Baker & Taylor Publisher Services